Dharmatrata Bkah-hgyur

Udânavarga

A collection of verses from the Buddhist canon

Dharmatrata Bkah-hgyur
Udânavarga
A collection of verses from the Buddhist canon
ISBN/EAN: 9783337231613

Printed in Europe, USA, Canada, Australia, Japan

Cover: Foto ©Lupo / pixelio.de

More available books at **www.hansebooks.com**

TRÜBNER'S ORIENTAL SERIES.

"A knowledge of the commonplace, at least, of Oriental literature, philosophy, and religion is as necessary to the general reader of the present day as an acquaintance with the Latin and Greek classics was a generation or so ago. Immense strides have been made within the present century in these branches of learning; Sanskrit has been brought within the range of accurate philology, and its invaluable ancient literature thoroughly investigated; the language and sacred books of the Zoroastrians have been laid bare; Egyptian, Assyrian, and other records of the remote past have been deciphered, and a group of scholars speak of still more recondite Accadian and Hittite monuments; but the results of all the scholarship that has been devoted to these subjects have been almost inaccessible to the public because they were contained for the most part in learned or expensive works, or scattered throughout the numbers of scientific periodicals. Messrs. TRÜBNER & CO., in a spirit of enterprise which does them infinite credit, have determined to supply the constantly-increasing want, and to give in a popular, or, at least, a comprehensive form, all this mass of knowledge to the world."—*Times*.

NOW READY,

Post 8vo, pp. 568, with Map, cloth, price 16s.

THE INDIAN EMPIRE: ITS HISTORY, PEOPLE, AND PRODUCTS.

Being a revised form of the article "India," in the "Imperial Gazetteer," remodelled into chapters, brought up to date, and incorporating the general results of the Census of 1881.

By W. W. HUNTER, C.I.E., LL.D.,

Director-General of Statistics to the Government of India.

"The article 'India,' in Volume IV., is the touchstone of the work, and proves clearly enough the sterling metal of which it is wrought. It represents the essence of the 100 volumes which contain the results of the statistical survey conducted by Dr. Hunter throughout each of the 240 districts of India. It is, moreover, the only attempt that has ever been made to show how the Indian people have been built up, and the evidence from the original materials has been for the first time sifted and examined by the light of the local research in which the author was for so long engaged."—*Times*.

THE FOLLOWING WORKS HAVE ALREADY APPEARED:—

Second Edition, post 8vo, cloth, pp. xvi.—428, price 16s.

ESSAYS ON THE SACRED LANGUAGE, WRITINGS, AND RELIGION OF THE PARSIS.

BY MARTIN HAUG, PH.D.,

Late of the Universities of Tübingen, Göttingen, and Bonn; Superintendent of Sanskrit Studies, and Professor of Sanskrit in the Poona College.

EDITED BY DR. E. W. WEST.

I. History of the Researches into the Sacred Writings and Religion of the Parsis, from the Earliest Times down to the Present.
II. Languages of the Parsi Scriptures.
III. The Zend-Avesta, or the Scripture of the Parsis.
IV. The Zoroastrian Religion, as to its Origin and Development.

"'Essays on the Sacred Language, Writings, and Religion of the Parsis,' by the late Dr. Martin Haug, edited by Dr. E. W. West. The author intended, on his return from India, to expand the materials contained in this work into a comprehensive account of the Zoroastrian religion, but the design was frustrated by his untimely death. We have, however, in a concise and readable form, a history of the researches into the sacred writings and religion of the Parsis from the earliest times down to the present—a dissertation on the languages of the Parsi Scriptures, a translation of the Zend-Avesta, or the Scripture of the Parsis, and a dissertation on the Zoroastrian religion, with especial reference to its origin and development."—*Times.*

Post 8vo, cloth, pp. viii.—176, price 7s. 6d.

TEXTS FROM THE BUDDHIST CANON

COMMONLY KNOWN AS "DHAMMAPADA."

With Accompanying Narratives.

Translated from the Chinese by S. BEAL, B.A., Professor of Chinese University College, London.

The Dhammapada, as hitherto known by the Pali Text Edition, as edited by Fausböll, by Max Müller's English, and Albrecht Weber's German translations, consists only of twenty-six chapters or sections, whilst the Chinese version, or rather recension, as now translated by Mr. Beal, consists of thirty-nine sections. The students of Pali who possess Fausböll's text, or either of the above-named translations, will therefore needs want Mr. Beal's English rendering of the Chinese version; the thirteen above-named additional sections not being accessible to them in any other form; for, even if they understand Chinese, the Chinese original would be unobtainable by them.

"Mr. Beal's rendering of the Chinese translation is a most valuable aid to the critical study of the work. It contains authentic texts gathered from ancient canonical books, and generally connected with some incident in the history of Buddha. Their great interest, however, consists in the light which they throw upon everyday life in India at the remote period at which they were written, and upon the method of teaching adopted by the founder of the religion. The method employed was principally parable, and the simplicity of the tales and the excellence of the morals inculcated, as well as the strange hold which they have retained upon the minds of millions of people, make them a very remarkable study."—*Times.*

"Mr. Beal, by making it accessible in an English dress, has added to the great services he has already rendered to the comparative study of religious history."—*Academy.*

"Valuable as exhibiting the doctrine of the Buddhists in its purest, least adulterated form, it brings the modern reader face to face with that simple creed and rule of conduct which won its way over the minds of myriads, and which is now nominally professed by 145 millions, who have overlaid its austere simplicity with innumerable ceremonies, forgotten its maxims, perverted its teaching, and so inverted its leading principle that a religion whose founder denied a God, now worships that founder as a god himself."—*Scotsman.*

Second Edition, post 8vo, cloth, pp. xxiv.—360, price 10s. 6d.

THE HISTORY OF INDIAN LITERATURE.

By ALBRECHT WEBER.

Translated from the Second German Edition by JOHN MANN, M.A., and THÉODOR ZACHARIAE, Ph.D., with the sanction of the Author.

Dr. BUHLER, Inspector of Schools in India, writes:—"When I was Professor of Oriental Languages in Elphinstone College, I frequently felt the want of such a work to which I could refer the students."

Professor COWELL, of Cambridge, writes:—"It will be especially useful to the students in our Indian colleges and universities. I used to long for such a book when I was teaching in Calcutta. Hindu students are intensely interested in the history of Sanskrit literature, and this volume will supply them with all they want on the subject."

Professor WHITNEY, Yale College, Newhaven, Conn., U.S.A., writes:— "I was one of the class to whom the work was originally given in the form of academic lectures. At their first appearance they were by far the most learned and able treatment of their subject; and with their recent additions they still maintain decidedly the same rank."

"Is perhaps the most comprehensive and lucid survey of Sanskrit literature extant. The essays contained in the volume were originally delivered as academic lectures, and at the time of their first publication were acknowledged to be by far the most learned and able treatment of the subject. They have now been brought up to date by the addition of all the most important results of recent research."— *Times.*

Post 8vo, cloth, pp. xii.—198, accompanied by Two Language Maps, price 12s.

A SKETCH OF
THE MODERN LANGUAGES OF THE EAST INDIES.

By ROBERT N. CUST.

The Author has attempted to fill up a vacuum, the inconvenience of which pressed itself on his notice. Much had been written about the languages of the East Indies, but the extent of our present knowledge had not even been brought to a focus. It occurred to him that it might be of use to others to publish in an arranged form the notes which he had collected for his own edification.

"Supplies a deficiency which has long been felt."—*Times.*

"The book before us is then a valuable contribution to philological science. It passes under review a vast number of languages, and it gives, or professes to give, in every case the sum and substance of the opinions and judgments of the best-informed writers."—*Saturday Review.*

Second Corrected Edition, post 8vo, pp. xii.—116, cloth, price 5s.

THE BIRTH OF THE WAR-GOD.

A Poem. By KALIDASA.

Translated from the Sanskrit into English Verse by RALPH T. H. GRIFFITH, M.A.

"A very spirited rendering of the *Kumárasambhava*, which was first published twenty-six years ago, and which we are glad to see made once more accessible."— *Times.*

"Mr. Griffith's very spirited rendering is well known to most who are at all interested in Indian literature, or enjoy the tenderness of feeling and rich creative imagination of its author."—*Indian Antiquary.*

"We are very glad to welcome a second edition of Professor Griffith's admirable translation. Few translations deserve a second edition better."—*Athenæum.*

Post 8vo, cloth, pp. 432, price 16s.

A CLASSICAL DICTIONARY OF HINDU MYTHOLOGY AND RELIGION, GEOGRAPHY, HISTORY, AND LITERATURE.

By JOHN DOWSON, M.R.A.S.,
Late Professor of Hindustani, Staff College.

In this work an endeavour has been made to supply the long-felt want of a Hindu Classical Dictionary. The main portion of this work consists of mythology, but religion is bound up with mythology, and in many points the two are quite inseparable.

This work will be a book of reference for all concerned in the government of the Hindus, but it will be more especially useful to young Civil Servants, and to masters and students in the universities, colleges, and schools in India.

"This not only forms an indispensable book of reference to students of Indian literature, but is also of great general interest, as it gives in a concise and easily accessible form all that need be known about the personages of Hindu mythology whose names are so familiar, but of whom so little is known outside the limited circle of *savants*."—*Times*.

"It is no slight gain when such subjects are treated fairly and fully in a moderate space; and we need only add that the few wants which we may hope to see supplied in new editions detract but little from the general excellence of Mr. Dowson's work."—*Saturday Review*.

Post 8vo, with View of Mecca, pp. cxii.–172, cloth, price 9s.

SELECTIONS FROM THE KORAN.

By EDWARD WILLIAM LANE,
Hon. Doctor of Literature, Leyden, &c., &c.; Translator of "The Thousand and One Nights;" &c., &c.

A New Edition, Revised and Enlarged, with an Introduction by
STANLEY LANE POOLE.

"... Has been long esteemed in this country as the compilation of one of the greatest Arabic scholars of the time, the late Mr. Lane, the well-known translator of the 'Arabian Nights.' ... The present editor has enhanced the value of his relative's work by divesting the text of a great deal of extraneous matter introduced by way of comment, and prefixing an introduction."—*Times*.

"Mr. Poole is both a generous and a learned biographer. ... Mr. Poole tells us the facts ... so far as it is possible for industry and criticism to ascertain them, and for literary skill to present them in a condensed and readable form."—*Englishman, Calcutta*.

Post 8vo, pp. vi.–368, cloth, price 14s.

MODERN INDIA AND THE INDIANS,

BEING A SERIES OF IMPRESSIONS, NOTES, AND ESSAYS.

By MONIER WILLIAMS, D.C.L.,
Hon. LL.D. of the University of Calcutta, Hon. Member of the Bombay Asiatic Society, Boden Professor of Sanskrit in the University of Oxford.

Third Edition, revised and augmented by considerable Additions, with Illustrations and a Map.

This edition will be found a great improvement on those that preceded it. The author has taken care to avail himself of all such criticisms on particular passages in the previous editions as appeared to him to be just, and he has enlarged the work by more than a hundred pages of additional matter.

"In this volume we have the thoughtful impressions of a thoughtful man on some of the most important questions connected with our Indian Empire. ... An enlightened observant man, travelling among an enlightened observant people, Professor Monier Williams has brought before the public in a pleasant form more of the manners and customs of the Queen's Indian subjects than we ever remember to have seen in any one work. He not only deserves the thanks of every Englishman for this able contribution to the study of Modern India—a subject with which we should be specially familiar—but he deserves the thanks of every Indian, Parsee or Hindu, Buddhist and Moslem, for his clear exposition of their manners, their creeds, and their necessities."—*Times*.

Post 8vo, pp. xliv.—376, cloth, price 14s.

METRICAL TRANSLATIONS FROM SANSKRIT WRITERS.

With an Introduction, many Prose Versions, and Parallel Passages from Classical Authors.

By J. MUIR, C.I.E., D.C.L., LL.D., Ph.D.

". . . An agreeable introduction to Hindu poetry."—*Times.*

". . . A volume which may be taken as a fair illustration alike of the religious and moral sentiments and of the legendary lore of the best Sanskrit writers."—*Edinburgh Daily Review.*

In Two Volumes, post 8vo, pp. viii.—408 and viii.—348, cloth, price 28s.

MISCELLANEOUS ESSAYS RELATING TO INDIAN SUBJECTS.

By BRIAN HOUGHTON HODGSON, Esq., F.R.S.,

Late of the Bengal Civil Service; Corresponding Member of the Institute; Chevalier of the Legion of Honour; late British Minister at the Court of Nepál, &c., &c.

CONTENTS OF VOL. I.

SECTION I.—On the Kocch, Bódó, and Dhimál Tribes.—Part I. Vocabulary.—Part II. Grammar.—Part III. Their Origin, Location, Numbers, Creed, Customs, Character, and Condition, with a General Description of the Climate they dwell in.—Appendix.

SECTION II.—On Himalayan Ethnology.—I. Comparative Vocabulary of the Languages of the Broken Tribes of Nepál.—II. Vocabulary of the Dialects of the Kiranti Language.—III. Grammatical Analysis of the Váyu Language. The Váyu Grammar.—IV. Analysis of the Báhing Dialect of the Kiranti Language. The Báhing Grammar.—V. On the Váyu or Hayu Tribe of the Central Himaláya.—VI. On the Kiranti Tribe of the Central Himaláya.

CONTENTS OF VOL. II.

SECTION III.—On the Aborigines of North-Eastern India. Comparative Vocabulary of the Tibetan, Bódó, and Gáró Tongues.

SECTION IV.—Aborigines of the North-Eastern Frontier.

SECTION V.—Aborigines of the Eastern Frontier.

SECTION VI.—The Indo-Chinese Borderers, and their connection with the Himalayans and Tibetans. Comparative Vocabulary of Indo-Chinese Borderers in Arakan. Comparative Vocabulary of Indo-Chinese Borderers in Tenasserim.

SECTION VII.—The Mongolian Affinities of the Caucasians.—Comparison and Analysis of Caucasian and Mongolian Words.

SECTION VIII.—Physical Type of Tibetans.

SECTION IX.—The Aborigines of Central India.—Comparative Vocabulary of the Aboriginal Languages of Central India.—Aborigines of the Eastern Ghats.—Vocabulary of some of the Dialects of the Hill and Wandering Tribes in the Northern Sircars.—Aborigines of the Nilgiris, with Remarks on their Affinities.—Supplement to the Nilgirian Vocabularies.—The Aborigines of Southern India and Ceylon.

SECTION X.—Route of Nepalese Mission to Pekin, with Remarks on the Water-Shed and Plateau of Tibet.

SECTION XI.—Route from Káthmándú, the Capital of Nepál, to Darjeeling in Sikim.—Memorandum relative to the Seven Cosis of Nepál.

SECTION XII.—Some Accounts of the Systems of Law and Police as recognised in the State of Nepál.

SECTION XIII.—The Native Method of making the Paper denominated Hindustan, Népálese.

SECTION XIV.—Pre-eminence of the Vernaculars; or, the Anglicists Answered: Being Letters on the Education of the People of India.

"For the study of the less-known races of India Mr. Brian Hodgson's 'Miscellaneous Essays' will be found very valuable both to the philologist and the ethnologist."—*Times.*

TRÜBNER'S ORIENTAL SERIES.

Third Edition, Two Vols., post 8vo, pp. viii.—268 and viii.—326, cloth, price 21s.

THE LIFE OR LEGEND OF GAUDAMA,

THE BUDDHA OF THE BURMESE. With Annotations.

The Ways to Neibban, and Notice on the Phongyies or Burmese Monks.

BY THE RIGHT REV. P. BIGANDET,

Bishop of Ramatha, Vicar-Apostolic of Ava and Pegu.

"The work is furnished with copious notes, which not only illustrate the subject-matter, but form a perfect encyclopædia of Buddhist lore."—*Times.*

"A work which will furnish European students of Buddhism with a most valuable help in the prosecution of their investigations."—*Edinburgh Daily Review.*

"Bishop Bigandet's invaluable work, . . . and no work founded—rather translated—from original sources presents to the Western student a more faithful picture than that of Bishop Bigandet."—*Indian Antiquary.*

"Viewed in this light, its importance is sufficient to place students of the subject under a deep obligation to its author."—*Calcutta Review.*

"This work is one of the greatest authorities upon Buddhism."—*Dublin Review.*

". . . A performance the great value of which is well known to all students of Buddhism."—*Tablet.*

Post 8vo, pp. xxiv.—420, cloth, price 18s.

CHINESE BUDDHISM.

A VOLUME OF SKETCHES, HISTORICAL AND CRITICAL.

BY J. EDKINS, D.D.

Author of "China's Place in Philology," "Religion in China," &c. &c.

"It contains a vast deal of important information on the subject, such as is only to be gained by long-continued study on the spot."—*Athenæum.*

"It is impossible within our limits even to mention the various subjects connected with Buddhism with which Dr. Edkins deals."—*Saturday Review.*

"Upon the whole, we know of no work comparable to it for the extent of its original research, and the simplicity with which this complicated system of philosophy, religion, literature, and ritual is set forth."—*British Quarterly Review.*

"The whole volume is replete with learning. . . . It deserves most careful study from all interested in the history of the religions of the world, and expressly of those who are concerned in the propagation of Christianity. Dr. Edkins notices in terms of just condemnation the exaggerated praise bestowed upon Buddhism by recent English writers."—*Record.*

Second Edition, post 8vo, pp. xxvi.—244, cloth, price 10s. 6d.

THE GULISTAN;

OR, ROSE GARDEN OF SHEKH MUSHLIU'D-DIN SADI OF SHIRAZ.

Translated for the First Time into Prose and Verse, with an Introductory Preface, and a Life of the Author, from the Atish Kadah,

BY EDWARD B. EASTWICK, C.B., M.A., F.R.S., M.R.A.S.,

Of Merton College, Oxford, &c.

"It is a very fair rendering of the original."—*Times.*

"The new edition has long been desired, and will be welcomed by all who take any interest in Oriental poetry. The *Gulistan* is a typical Persian verse-book of the highest order. Mr. Eastwick's rhymed translation . . . has long established itself in a secure position as the best version of Sadi's finest work."—*Academy.*

"It is both faithfully and gracefully executed."—*Tablet.*

Post 8vo, pp. 496, cloth, price 18s.

LINGUISTIC AND ORIENTAL ESSAYS.

WRITTEN FROM THE YEAR 1846 TO 1878.

BY ROBERT NEEDHAM CUST,

Late Member of Her Majesty's Indian Civil Service; Hon. Secretary to
the Royal Asiatic Society;
and Author of "The Modern Languages of the East Indies."

"We know none who has described Indian life, especially the life of the natives, with so much learning, sympathy, and literary talent."—*Academy.*

"It is impossible to do justice to any of these essays in the space at our command... But they seem to us to be full of suggestive and original remarks."—*St. James's Gazette.*

"His book contains a vast amount of information, ... of much interest to every intelligent reader. It is, he tells us, the result of thirty-five years of inquiry, reflection, and speculation, and that on subjects as full of fascination as of food for thought."—*Tablet.*

"The essays . . . . . exhibit such a thorough acquaintance with the history and antiquities of India as to entitle him to speak as one having authority."—*Edinburgh Daily Review.*

"The author speaks with the authority of personal experience. . . . . It is this constant association with the country and the people which gives such a vividness to many of the pages."—*Athenæum.*

Post 8vo, pp. civ.—348, cloth, price 18s.

BUDDHIST BIRTH STORIES; or, Jataka Tales.

The Oldest Collection of Folk-lore Extant:

BEING THE JATAKATTHAVANNANA,

For the first time Edited in the original Pāli.

BY V. FAUSBOLL;
And Translated by T. W. RHYS DAVIDS.

Translation. Volume I.

"These are tales supposed to have been told by the Buddha of what he had seen and heard in his previous births. They are probably the nearest representatives of the original Aryan stories from which sprang the folk-lore of Europe as well as India, and from which the Semitic nations also borrowed much. The introduction contains a most interesting disquisition on the migrations of these fables, tracing their reappearance in the various groups of folk-lore legends respectively known as 'Æsop's Fables,' the 'Hitopadesa,' the Calilag and Damnag series, and even 'The Arabian Nights.' Among other old friends, we meet with a version of the Judgment of Solomon, which proves, after all, to be an Aryan, and not a Semitic tale."—*Times.*

"It is now some years since Mr. Rhys Davids asserted his right to be heard on this subject by his able article on Buddhism in the new edition of the 'Encyclopædia Britannica.'"—*Leeds Mercury.*

"All who are interested in Buddhist literature ought to feel deeply indebted to Mr. Rhys Davids. His well-established reputation as a Pali scholar is a sufficient guarantee for the fidelity of his version, and the style of his translations is deserving of high praise."—*Academy.*

"It is certain that no more competent expositor of Buddhism could be found than Mr. Rhys Davids, and that these Birth Stories will be of the greatest interest and importance to students. In the Jātaka book we have, then, a priceless record of the earliest imaginative literature of our race; and Mr. Rhys Davids is well warranted in claiming that it presents to us a nearly complete picture of the social life and customs and popular beliefs of the common people of Aryan tribes, closely related to ourselves, just as they were passing through the first stages of civilisation."—*St. James's Gazette.*

Post 8vo, pp. xxviii.—362, cloth, price 14s.

A TALMUDIC MISCELLANY;

OR, A THOUSAND AND ONE EXTRACTS FROM THE TALMUD, THE MIDRASHIM, AND THE KABBALAH.

Compiled and Translated by PAUL ISAAC HERSHON,
Author of "Genesis According to the Talmud," &c.

With Notes and Copious Indexes.

"To obtain in so concise and handy a form as this volume a general idea of the Talmud is a boon to Christians at least."—*Times.*

"This is a new volume of the 'Oriental Series,' and its peculiar and popular character will make it attractive to general readers. Mr. Hershon is a very competent scholar.... The present selection contains samples of the good, bad, and indifferent, and especially extracts that throw light upon the Scriptures. The extracts have been all derived, word for word, and made at first hand, and references are carefully given."—*British Quarterly Review.*

"Mr. Hershon's book, at all events, will convey to English readers a more complete and truthful notion of the Talmud than any other work that has yet appeared."—*Daily News.*

"Without overlooking in the slightest the several attractions of the previous volumes of the 'Oriental Series,' we have no hesitation in saying that this surpasses them all in interest."—*Edinburgh Daily Review.*

"Mr. Hershon has done this; he has taken samples from all parts of the Talmud, and thus given English readers what is, we believe, a fair set of specimens which they can test for themselves."—*The Record.*

"Altogether we believe that this book is by far the best fitted in the present state of knowledge to enable the general reader or the ordinary student to gain a fair and unbiassed conception of the multifarious contents of the wonderful miscellany which can only be truly understood—so Jewish pride asserts—by the life-long devotion of scholars of the Chosen People."—*Inquirer.*

"The value and importance of this volume consist in the fact that scarcely a single extract is given in its pages but throws some light, direct or refracted, upon those Scriptures which are the common heritage of Jew and Christian alike."—*John Bull.*

"His acquaintance with the Talmud, &c., is seen on every page of his book... It is a capital specimen of Hebrew scholarship; a monument of learned, loving, light-giving labour."—*Jewish Herald.*

Post 8vo, pp. xii.—228, cloth, price 7s. 6d.

THE CLASSICAL POETRY OF THE JAPANESE.

BY BASIL HALL CHAMBERLAIN,
Author of "Yeigo Heñkaku Shirañ."

"A very curious volume. The author has manifestly devoted much labour to the task of studying the poetical literature of the Japanese, and rendering characteristic specimens into English verse."—*Daily News.*

"Mr. Chamberlain's volume is, so far as we are aware, the first attempt which has been made to interpret the literature of the Japanese to the western world. It is to the classical poetry of Old Japan that we must turn for indigenous Japanese thought, and in the volume before us we have a selection from that poetry rendered into graceful English verse."—*Tablet.*

"It is undoubtedly one of the best translations of lyric literature which has appeared during the close of the last year."—*Celestial Empire.*

"Mr. Chamberlain set himself a difficult task when he undertook to reproduce Japanese poetry in an English form. But he has evidently laboured *con amore*, and his efforts are successful to a degree."—*London and China Express.*

Post 8vo, pp. xii.—164, cloth, price 10s. 6d.

THE HISTORY OF ESARHADDON (Son of Sennacherib),

KING OF ASSYRIA, B.C. 681–668.

Translated from the Cuneiform Inscriptions upon Cylinders and Tablets in the British Museum Collection; together with a Grammatical Analysis of each Word, Explanations of the Ideographs by Extracts from the Bi-Lingual Syllabaries, and List of Eponyms, &c.

By ERNEST A. BUDGE, B.A., M.R.A.S.,

Assyrian Exhibitioner, Christ's College, Cambridge, Member of the Society of Biblical Archæology.

"Students of scriptural archæology will also appreciate the 'History of Esarhaddon.'"—*Times.*

"There is much to attract the scholar in this volume. It does not pretend to popularise studies which are yet in their infancy. Its primary object is to translate, but it does not assume to be more than tentative, and it offers both to the professed Assyriologist and to the ordinary non-Assyriological Semitic scholar the means of controlling its results."—*Academy.*

"Mr. Budge's book is, of course, mainly addressed to Assyrian scholars and students. They are not, it is to be feared, a very numerous class. But the more thanks are due to him on that account for the way in which he has acquitted himself in his laborious task."—*Tablet.*

Post 8vo, pp. 448, cloth, price 21s.

THE MESNEVI

(Usually known as THE MESNEVIYI SHERIF, or HOLY MESNEVI

OF

MEVLANA (OUR LORD) JELALU 'D-DIN MUHAMMED ER-RUMI.

Book the First.

Together with some Account of the Life and Acts of the Author, of his Ancestors, and of his Descendants.

Illustrated by a Selection of Characteristic Anecdotes, as Collected by their Historian,

MEVLANA SHEMSU-'D-DIN AHMED, EL EFLAKI, EL 'ARIFI.

Translated, and the Poetry Versified, in English,

By JAMES W. REDHOUSE, M.R.A.S., &c.

"A complete treasury of occult Oriental lore."—*Saturday Review.*
"This book will be a very valuable help to the reader ignorant of Persia, who is desirous of obtaining an insight into a very important department of the literature extant in that language."—*Tablet.*

Post 8vo, pp. xvi.—280, cloth, price 6s.

EASTERN PROVERBS AND EMBLEMS

ILLUSTRATING OLD TRUTHS.

By REV. J. LONG,

Member of the Bengal Asiatic Society, F.R.G.S.

"We regard the book as valuable, and wish for it a wide circulation and attentive reading."—*Record.*
"Altogether, it is quite a feast of good things."—*Globe.*
"Is full of interesting matter."—*Antiquary.*

Post 8vo, pp. viii.—270, cloth, price 7s. 6d.

INDIAN POETRY;

Containing a New Edition of the "Indian Song of Songs," from the Sanscrit of the "Gita Govinda" of Jayadeva; Two Books from "The Iliad of India" (Mahabharata), "Proverbial Wisdom" from the Shlokas of the Hitopadesa, and other Oriental Poems.

By EDWIN ARNOLD, C.S.I., Author of "The Light of Asia."

"In this new volume of Messrs. Trübner's Oriental Series, Mr. Edwin Arnold does good service by illustrating, through the medium of his musical English melodies, the power of Indian poetry to stir European emotions. The 'Indian Song of Songs' is not unknown to scholars. Mr. Arnold will have introduced it among popular English poems. Nothing could be more graceful and delicate than the shades by which Krishna is portrayed in the gradual process of being weaned by the love of

'Beautiful Radha, jasmine-bosomed Radha,'

from the allurements of the forest nymphs, in whom the five senses are typified."—*Times.*

"The studious reader of Mr. Arnold's verse will have added richly to his store of Oriental knowledge . . . infused in every page of this delightful volume. . . . No other English poet has ever thrown his genius and his art so thoroughly into the work of translating Eastern ideas as Mr. Arnold has done in his splendid paraphrases of language contained in these mighty epics."—*Daily Telegraph.*

"The poem abounds with imagery of Eastern luxuriousness and sensuousness; the air seems laden with the spicy odours of the tropics, and the verse has a richness and a melody sufficient to captivate the senses of the dullest."—*Standard.*

"The translator, while producing a very enjoyable poem, has adhered with tolerable fidelity to the original text."—*Overland Mail.*

"We certainly wish Mr. Arnold success in his attempt 'to popularise Indian classics,' that being, as his preface tells us, the goal towards which he bends his efforts."—*Allen's Indian Mail.*

Post 8vo, pp. 336, cloth, price 16s.,

THE RELIGIONS OF INDIA.

By A. BARTH.

Translated from the French with the authority and assistance of the Author.

The author has, at the request of the publishers, considerably enlarged the work for the translator, and has added the literature of the subject to date; the translation may, therefore, be looked upon as an equivalent of a new and improved edition of the original.

"This last addition to Messrs. Trübner's 'Oriental Series' is not only a valuable manual of the religions of India, which marks a distinct step in the treatment of the subject, but also a useful work of reference."—*Academy.*

"This volume is a reproduction, with corrections and additions, of an article contributed by the learned author two years ago to the 'Encyclopédie des Sciences Religieuses.' It attracted much notice when it first appeared, and is generally admitted to present the best summary extant of the vast subject with which it deals."—*Tablet.*

"This is not only on the whole the best but the only manual of the religions of India, apart from Buddhism, which we have in English. The present work is in every way worthy of the promising school of young French scholars to which the author belongs, and shows not only great knowledge of the facts and power of clear exposition, but also great insight into the inner history and the deeper meaning of the great religion, for it is in reality only one, which it proposes to describe."—*Modern Review.*

"The merit of the work has been emphatically recognised by the most authoritative Orientalists, both in this country and on the continent of Europe, and Messrs. Trübner have done well in adding it to their 'Oriental Series.' But probably there are few Indianists (if we may use the word) who would not derive a good deal of information from it, and especially from the extensive bibliography provided in the notes."—*Dublin Review.*

". . . . Such a sketch M. Barth has drawn with a master hand, and his bold, clear method of treating his difficult subject is scarcely marred by a translation which would have rendered a less perspicuous style utterly incomprehensible."—*Critic (New York).*

Post 8vo, pp. viii.—152, cloth, price 6s.
HINDU PHILOSOPHY.
The Sānkhya Kārika of Is'wara Krishna.
An Exposition of the System of Kapila, with an Appendix on the Nyāya and Vais'eshika Systems.

By JOHN DAVIES, M.A. (Cantab.), M.R.A.S.

The system of Kapila is the earliest attempt on record to give an answer from reason alone to the mysterious questions which arise in every thoughtful mind about the origin of the world, the nature and relations of man and his future destiny. It contains nearly all that India has produced in the department of pure philosophy. Other systems, though classed as philosophic, are mainly devoted to logic and physical science, or to an exposition of the Vedas.

"Such a combination of words is discouraging to the non-Orientalist, but fortunately for him he finds in Mr. Davies a patient and learned guide who leads him into the intricacies of the philosophy of India, and supplies him with a clue, that he may not be lost in them—nay more, points out to him the similarity between the speculations of the remote East and of modern Germany, however much they may differ in external appearance. In the preface he states that the system of Kapila is the 'earliest attempt on record to give an answer, from reason alone, to the mysterious questions which arise in every thoughtful mind about the origin of the world, the nature and relations of man and his future destiny,' and in his learned and able notes he exhibits 'the connection of the Sankhya system with the philosophy of Spinoza,' and 'the connection of the system of Kapila with that of Schopenhauer and Von Hartmann.'"—*Foreign Church Chronicle.*

"Mr. Davies's volume on Hindu Philosophy is an undoubted gain to all students of the development of thought. The system of Kapila which, is here given in a translation from the Sānkhya Kārikā, is the only contribution of India to pure philosophy. The older system of Kapila, however, though it could never have been very widely accepted or understood, presents many points of deep interest to the student of comparative philosophy, and without Mr. Davies's lucid interpretation it would be difficult to appreciate these points in any adequate manner."—*Saturday Review.*

"We welcome Mr. Davies's book as a valuable addition to our philosophical library."—*Notes and Queries.*

Post 8vo, pp. xvi.—296, cloth, price 10s. 6d.
THE MIND OF MENCIUS;
Or, POLITICAL ECONOMY FOUNDED UPON MORAL PHILOSOPHY.

A Systematic Digest of the Doctrines of the Chinese Philosopher Mencius.

Translated from the Original Text and Classified, with Comments and Explanations,

By the Rev. ERNST FABER, Rhenish Mission Society.

Translated from the German, with Additional Notes,

By the Rev. A. B. HUTCHINSON, C.M.S., Church Mission, Hong Kong, Author of "Chinese Primer, Old Testament History."

"The Mind of Mencius" is a Translation from the German of one of the most original and useful works on Chinese Philosophy ever published.

"Mr. Faber is already well known in the field of Chinese studies by his digest of the doctrines of Confucius. In the present volume he gives us a systematic digest of those of Mencius, the greatest and most popular of the disciples of Confucius. The value of this work will be perceived when it is remembered that at no time since relations commenced between China and the West has the former been so powerful—we had almost said aggressive—as now. For those who will give it careful study, Mr. Faber's work is one of the most valuable of the excellent series to which it belongs."—*Nature.*

Post 8vo, pp. x.—130, cloth, price 6s.

A MANUAL OF HINDU PANTHEISM. VEDÂNTASÂRA.

Translated, with copious Annotations, by MAJOR G. A. JACOB,
Bombay Staff Corps; Inspector of Army Schools.

The design of this little work is to provide for missionaries, and for others who, like them, have little leisure for original research, an accurate summary of the doctrines of the Vedânta.

"There can be no question that the religious doctrines most widely held by the people of India are mainly Pantheistic. And of Hindu Pantheism, at all events in its most modern phases, its Vedântasâra presents the best summary. But then this work is a mere summary: a skeleton, the dry bones of which require to be clothed with skin and bones, and to be animated by vital breath before the ordinary reader will discern in it a living reality. Major Jacob, therefore, has wisely added to his translation of the Vedântasâra copious notes from the writings of well-known Oriental scholars, in which he has, we think, elucidated all that required elucidation. So that the work, as here presented to us, presents no difficulties which a very moderate amount of application will not overcome."—*Tablet.*

"The modest title of Major Jacob's work conveys but an inadequate idea of the vast amount of research embodied in his notes to the text of the Vedântasâra. So copious, indeed, are these, and so much collateral matter do they bring to bear on the subject, that the diligent student will rise from their perusal with a fairly adequate view of Hindû philosophy generally. It is, perhaps, to be regretted that the author has not confined himself to exposition, and left his readers to form their own opinion of the value of the tenets described. But this is the only fault we have to find with his book, which, in other respects, is one of the best of its kind that we have seen."—*Calcutta Review.*

Post 8vo, pp. xii.—154, cloth, price 7s. 6d.

TSUNI—||GOAM:

THE SUPREME BEING OF THE KHOI-KHOI.

BY THEOPHILUS HAHN, Ph.D.,

Custodian of the Grey Collection, Cape Town; Corresponding Member of the Geogr. Society, Dresden; Corresponding Member of the Anthropological Society, Vienna, &c., &c.

"The first instalment of Dr. Hahn's labours will be of interest, not at the Cape only, but in every University of Europe. It is, in fact, a most valuable contribution to the comparative study of religion and mythology. Accounts of their religion and mythology were scattered about in various books; these have been carefully collected by Dr. Hahn and printed in his second chapter, enriched and improved by what he has been able to collect himself."—*Prof. Max Müller in the Nineteenth Century.*

"Dr. Hahn's book is that of a man who is both a philologist and believer in philological methods, and a close student of savage manners and customs."—*Saturday Review.*

"It is full of good things. Wherever you put in your thumb you are pretty certain to pull out a plum."—*St. James's Gazette.*

In Two Volumes. Vol. I., post 8vo, pp. xii.—392, cloth, price 12s. 6d.

A COMPREHENSIVE COMMENTARY TO THE QURAN.

TO WHICH IS PREFIXED SALE'S PRELIMINARY DISCOURSE, WITH
ADDITIONAL NOTES AND EMENDATIONS.

Together with a Complete Index to the Text, Preliminary Discourse, and Notes.

By Rev. E. M. WHERRY, M.A., Lodiana.

"As Mr. Wherry's book is intended for missionaries in India, it is no doubt well that they should be prepared to meet, if they can, the ordinary arguments and interpretations, and for this purpose Mr. Wherry's additions will prove useful."—*Saturday Review.*

Post 8vo, pp. 96, cloth, price 5s.

THE QUATRAINS OF OMAR KHAYYAM.

Translated by E. H. WHINFIELD, M.A.,
Barrister-at-Law, late H.M. Bengal Civil Service.

Omar Khayyám (the tent-maker) was born about the middle of the fifth century of the Hejirah, corresponding to the eleventh of the Christian era, in the neighbourhood of Naishapur, the capital of Khorasán, and died in 517 A.H. (=1122 A.D.)

"Mr. Whinfield has executed a difficult task with considerable success, and his version contains much that will be new to those who only know Mr. Fitzgerald's delightful selection."—*Academy.*

"There are several editions of the Quatrains, varying greatly in their readings. Mr. Whinfield has used three of these for his excellent translation. The most prominent features in the Quatrains are their profound agnosticism, combined with a fatalism based more on philosophic than religious grounds, their Epicureanism and the spirit of universal tolerance and charity which animates them."—*Calcutta Review.*

Post 8vo, pp. xii.—302, cloth, price 8s. 6d.

YUSUF AND ZULAIKHA.

A POEM BY JAMI.

Translated from the Persian into English Verse.

By RALPH T. H. GRIFFITH.

"Mr. Griffith, who has done already good service as translator into verse from the Sanscrit, has done further good work in this translation from the Persian, which forms part of 'Trübner's Oriental Series;' and he has evidently shown not a little skill in his rendering the quaint and very oriental style of his author into our more prosaic, less figurative, language. . . . The work, besides its intrinsic merits, is of importance as being one of the most popular and famous poems of Persia, and that which is read in all the independent native schools of India where Persian is taught. It is as interesting, also, as a striking instance of the manner in which the stories of the Jews have been transformed and added to by tradition among the Mahometans, who look upon Joseph as 'the ideal of manly beauty and more than manly virtue;' and, indeed, in this poem he seems to be endowed with almost divine, or at any rate angelic, gifts and excellence."—*Scotsman.*

In Two Volumes. Vol. I., post 8vo, pp. xxiv.—230, cloth, price 7s. 6d.

A COMPARATIVE HISTORY OF THE EGYPTIAN AND MESOPOTAMIAN RELIGIONS.

By Dr. C. P. TIELE.

Vol. I.—HISTORY OF THE EGYPTIAN RELIGION.

Translated from the Dutch with the Assistance of the Author.

By JAMES BALLINGAL.

"This latest addition to 'Trübner's Oriental Series' may not prove one of the most attractive; but it is one of the most scholarly, and it places in the hands of the English readers a history of Egyptian Religion which is very complete, which is based on the best materials, and which has been illustrated by the latest results of research. In this volume there is a great deal of information, as well as independent investigation, for the trustworthiness of which Dr. Tiele's name is in itself a guarantee; and the description of the successive religions under the Old Kingdom, the Middle Kingdom, and the New Kingdom, is given in a manner which is scholarly and minute."—*Scotsman.*

"The analysis of the remains of Egyptian antiquity, so far as the religion of the people is regarded, is well worth reading, and to it we must refer those of our readers who are interested in the subject."—*Tablet.*

"We trust that the present work will find sufficient support to encourage the early publication of the remaining portion, treating of the Babylonian-Assyrian religion, and of the religions of Phœnicia and Israel."—*National Reformer.*

Post 8vo, cloth, pp. ix.—281, price 10s. 6d.

THE SARVA-DARSANA-SAMGRAHA;
OR, REVIEW OF THE DIFFERENT SYSTEMS OF HINDU PHILOSOPHY,

BY MADHAVA ACHARYA.

Translated by E. B. COWELL, M.A., Professor of Sanskrit in the University of Cambridge, and A. E. GOUGH, M.A., Professor of Philosophy in the Presidency College, Calcutta.

This work is an interesting specimen of Hindu critical ability. The author successively passes in review the sixteen philosophical systems current in the fourteenth century in the South of India; and he gives what appears to him to be their most important tenets, and the principal arguments by which their followers endeavoured to maintain them; and he often displays some quaint humour as he throws himself for the time into the position of their advocate, and holds, as it were, a temporary brief on behalf of opinions entirely at variance with his own.

Post 8vo, cloth, pp. lxv.—368, price 14s.

TIBETAN TALES DERIVED FROM INDIAN SOURCES.
Translated from the Tibetan of the KAH-GYUR.
BY F. ANTON VON SCHIEFNER.

Done into English from the German, with an Introduction,

BY W. R. S. RALSTON, M.A.

Post 8vo, pp. viii.—266, cloth, price 9s.

LINGUISTIC ESSAYS.
BY CARL ABEL.

CONTENTS.

Language as the Expression of National Modes of Thought.	The Connection between Dictionary and Grammar.
The Conception of Love in some Ancient and Modern Languages.	The Possibility of a Common Literary Language for all Slavs.
The English Verbs of Command.	The Order and Position of Words in the Latin Sentence.
Semariology.	The Coptic Language.
Philological Methods.	

The Origin of Language.

Proving the signification of words and forms to reflect a nation's general view of the universe, the Author advocates a psychological study of language, to supplement the prevailing formalism of ordinary grammar. To this end English and other familiar linguistic notions are tested by a new method of national and international analysis, which combines the dictionary and the grammar; the origin of language and the primitive significance of sounds are unravelled in essays, containing striking results of etymological research; while in the connection between philology, psychology, and politics, the bearing of linguistic lore upon the general concerns of mankind is conclusively evidenced. The most enjoyable faculty in the exercise, but, frequently, the one least enjoyed in the study, speech, in these treatises, is shown to constitute at once the most faithful and the most attractive record of the history of the human, and, more especially, the national mind.

Post 8vo, pp. vi.—208, cloth, price 8s. 6d.
THE BHAGAVAD-GÎTÂ.
Translated, with Introduction and Notes,
By JOHN DAVIES, M.A. (Cantab.)

Post 8vo, pp. xxiv.—268, cloth, price 9s.
THE PHILOSOPHY OF THE UPANISHADS AND ANCIENT INDIAN METAPHYSICS.
As exhibited in a series of Articles contributed to the *Calcutta Review*.
By ARCHIBALD EDWARD GOUGH, M.A., Lincoln College, Oxford; Principal of the Calcutta Madrasa.

Post 8vo, pp. xvi.—224, cloth, price 9s.
UDÂNAVARGA.
A COLLECTION OF VERSES FROM THE BUDDHIST CANON.
Compiled by DHARMATRÂTA.
BEING THE NORTHERN BUDDHIST VERSION OF DHAMMAPADA.
Translated from the Tibetan of Bkah-hgyur, with Notes, and Extracts from the Commentary of Pradjnavarman,
By W. WOODVILLE ROCKHILL.

THE FOLLOWING WORKS ARE IN PREPARATION:—

Post 8vo, cloth.
THE ODES OF HAFIZ:
BEING A COMPLETE METRICAL TRANSLATION OF THE WORKS OF THE GREAT LYRIC POET OF PERSIA.
By E. H. PALMER, M.A., Lord Almoner's Professor of Arabic in the University of Cambridge.

Post 8vo.
THE SIX JEWELS OF THE LAW.
With Pali Texts and English Translation,
By R. MORRIS, LL.D.

In Two Volumes, post 8vo, cloth.
BUDDHIST RECORDS OF THE WESTERN WORLD,
BEING THE SI-YU-KI BY HWEN THSANG.
Translated from the Original Chinese, with Introduction, Index, &c.,
By SAMUEL BEAL,
Trinity College, Cambridge; Professor of Chinese, University College, London.

TRÜBNER'S ORIENTAL SERIES.

THE APHORISMS OF THE SANKHYA PHILOSOPHY OF KAPILA.

With Illustrative Extracts from the Commentaries.

By the late J. R. BALLANTYNE.

Second Edition. Edited by FITZEDWARD HALL.

Post 8vo, cloth.

MĀNAVA-DHARMA-CĀSTRA;

OR, LAWS OF MANU.

A New Translation, with Introduction, Notes, &c.

By A. C. BURNELL, Ph.D., C.I.E., a Foreign Member of the Royal Danish Academy, and Hon. Member of several Learned Societies.

The Author of this New Version, having long been a Judge in India, will pay particular attention to this book, as it is used in the Law Courts, &c. &c.

LONDON: TRÜBNER & CO., 57 AND 59 LUDGATE HILL.

PRINTED BY BALLANTYNE, HANSON AND CO.
EDINBURGH AND LONDON

TRÜBNER'S
ORIENTAL SERIES.

Ballantyne Press
BALLANTYNE, HANSON AND CO.
EDINBURGH AND LONDON

UDÂNAVARGA:

A Collection of Verses from the Buddhist Canon.

Compiled by DHARMATRÂTA.

being the

NORTHERN BUDDHIST VERSION OF DHAMMAPADA.

Translated from the Tibetan of the Bkah=hgyur.

WITH NOTES AND EXTRACTS FROM THE COMMENTARY OF PRADJNÂVARMAN.

by

W. WOODVILLE ROCKHILL.

LONDON:
TRÜBNER & CO., LUDGATE HILL.
1883.
[*All rights reserved.*]

TO

WILLIAM D. WHITNEY, Ph.D.,
PROFESSOR OF SANSKRIT IN YALE COLLEGE, NEW HAVEN.

This Work

IS RESPECTFULLY INSCRIBED,

AS A SLIGHT RECOGNITION OF HIS GREAT KINDNESS,

BY

THE TRANSLATOR.

INTRODUCTION.

THE text here translated is taken from vol. xxvi. of the sûtra section of the Bkah-hgyur, folios 329-400. This version has been revised on that of vol. lxxi. of the Bstan-hgyur, folios 1-53, which, though generally very incorrect reproducing nearly all the errors of the Bkah-hgyur (besides many others of its own), has enabled me to correct and complete my text in many places where it was so much effaced in the copy I made use of (that of the National Library at Paris) as to be nearly useless.

The work is divided into thirty-three chapters and four books, each of which contains about the same number of verses. Book I. has twelve chapters and 260 verses, Book II. twelve chapters and 249 verses, Book III. six chapters and 248 verses, Book IV. three chapters and 232 verses, making in all 989 verses or udânas, the greater part of which are in verses of seven and nine syllables.[1]

The title, "Tched-du brjod-pai tsoms," is rendered in Sanskrit by Udânavarga, *i.e.*, chapters of udânas, but the word udâna must not be understood to imply "joyous utterances, hymns of praise," but something nearly approaching "gâtha, verse, or stanza,"[2] although in some cases, where certain virtues are extolled, the word is employed with its habitual acceptation of "hymn."

Such verses are very generally found at the end of the sermons or sûtras of Gautama, and were probably intended

---

[1] There is really no prosody in Tibetan, metres being only distinguishable by the number of syllables in each line. In the Rgya-tcher-rol-pa (Lalita Vistara) I find 7, 9, 11, 13, 15, 17, and 21 syllabled lines, the first three being the most used.

[2] It would be perfectly admissible to call this work "a sûtra," using, however, that word in its habitual sense of "series of aphorisms." See L. Feer, Une Sentence du Buddha sur la Guerre, p. 34, note.

to convey to his hearers, in a few easily remembered lines, the essence of his teaching. It appears to me that the founder of Buddhism must have attached great importance to these verses, and that he advocated their use by all his disciples. Take, for example, the history of Çariputra's meeting with Açvadjit shortly after the former's conversion, and we see at once what a single gâtha was able to do in the eyes of early Buddhists, and what rôle these aphorisms undoubtedly played in the work of their missionaries. As a natural consequence of the importance attributed to these verses, it appeared desirable to the first successors of the Buddha to collect in separate works all such utterances of the Master as might prove especially instructive, and as best answering the purposes of their school. To this plan is undoubtedly due the fact that in both the Southern and Northern canons are numerous works which only contain the pith of more voluminous and older ones attributable to the Buddha. In the Northern canon we know of the Sûtra in 42 sections and the Udânavarga, besides several others in the extra-canonical collection (the Bstan-hgyur). The Southern canon offers us a much greater number of such works, the best known of which are the Dhammapada and the Sutta Nipâta.

The Udânavarga contains 300 verses, which are nearly identical with verses of the Dhammapada; 150 more resemble verses of that work; twenty are to be found in the Sutta Nipâta, and about the same number are very similar to parts of the same book. Thus more than half of the Udânavarga is found in works of the Southern canon, and it appears highly probable that if the Udâna, the Theragâthâ, Therigâthâ, &c., had been examined, many more of the verses of the Tibetan work would have been found in them.

If the Tibetan version has been constantly compared with the Pâli, it is not because I consider the latter as the text on which the Tibetan translation was made, but because it is the only term of comparison available.

INTRODUCTION.

Throughout this work there occur constant slight variations from the Páli, and, knowing as we do, the scrupulous care of the Indian Pandits who supervised the Tibetan translation,[1] it is not possible to admit that these differences are the result of carelessness, but rather we must explain them by the existence of different versions on which the Páli and the Northern Buddhist translations were made. Now, for example, in the Páli Nidânakathâ, p. 76, we find the two celebrated verses, 153, 154, of the Dhammapada. In both works these verses are the same in every respect, but in the Tibetan version of the Nidânakathâ, called the Jatakanidânam,[2] we find a quite different version of them. The text of the Udânavarga (chap. xxx. 6, 7) closely follows, however, the Páli version.

The version of the Jatakanidânam is as follows. "He sung this udâna, sung by all Buddhas:—

"153 Through an endless circle of births
Have I sought to end, to destroy the poison,
Seeking the maker of the house;
Again and again (have I known) the sorrow of birth.
154 I have found the maker of the house;
No more shall (he) make a house for me;
All his grief is pulverised,
And the poison is destroyed with the house.
(My) mind is freed from the sanskâra;
Craving is ended and (I) shall be no more."

This differs too much from the other versions to admit of the supposition of the translator having misunderstood the Páli "*sandhávissam, visamkhitam,*" &c., of the generally received text.

We might show similar discrepancies between gâthâs 133, 134, of the Nidânakathâ and the two Tibetan versions of the Jatakanidânam[3] and the Udânavarga, but what has been said appears sufficient to show that there must

---

[1] See Burnouf, Intr. à l'Hist., p. 25 *et pas.;* Foucaux, Rgya-tcher-rol-pa. *passim.*
[2] Bkah-hgyur, Mdo xxx. f. 520
[3] Jatakanidânam, *loc. cit.,* fol. 454b, and also fol. 458a, which corresponds with Nidânakathâ, p. 24, gâthâ 163.

have existed at an early date several versions of the Buddhist canon, and that the Pâli and the Tibetan translations were most likely made from texts that differed to some extent.

Our text affords no clue as to the language from which it was translated; it only gives the name of the work "in the language of the White Plain" or India. This expression is generally used to designate "Sanskrit;" it can, however, mean nothing more than Indian vernacular; and it is well known that at the time the Tibetan translations were made there existed Buddhist works in the language of Li (Khotan or Nepal), Zahora (Punjab), Kachmere,[1] &c., and that Pâli works were also made use of by the Indian translators, for quite a number of volumes of the Bkah-hgyur (notably vol. xxx. of the Mdo), contain texts directly translated from that language.[2] I am, however, inclined to think that it was made from a Sanskrit version in the dialect prevalent in Kachmere in the first century B.C., at which period and in which place the compiler, Dharmatrâta, probably lived.

The Udânavarga is found also in the Chinese Tripitaka. The title of the work is there "Chuh-yau-king," or Nidâna Sûtra.[3] It is also divided into thirty-three chapters, the titles of which agree with those of the Tibetan, with the following slight differences:—Chap. iv. is "Absence of Careless Behaviour;" chap. v. "Reflection;" chap. vi. "Intelligence;" chap. xxix. "The Twins" (*Yamaka*[4]). The contents of the two works, as far as has been ascertained, are identical.

Both the Chinese and the Tibetan version attribute the compilation of the Udânavarga to Dharmatrâta,[5] and the

---

[1] See Schlaginweit's Könige von Tibet, fol. 20b.
[2] See L. Feer, Annales du Musée Guimet, ii. p. 288.
[3] See Beal, Catalogue, p. 85.
[4] I am indebted to Mr. Beal for this information. The title of chap. xxix. of the Tibetan version might also be translated by *Yamaka*, if night and day are considered as forming a pair.
[5] Csoma in As. Res. xx. p. 477, and M. Feer, Annales du Musée Guimet, ii. p. 280, call him Dharmarakshita, which in Tibetan would be *Tchos skyong*, whereas the name is translated by *Tchos skyob*.

former says that he was the uncle of Vasumitra. If this Vasumitra was the one who was president of the Synod held under Kanishka, we might at once assign Dharmatrâta to the first century B.C. Unfortunately the question cannot be solved so easily. Târanâtha says that there was a Sthavira Dharmatrâta, who was one of the leaders of the Vaibâshika, "but," he adds, "one must not confound this Dharmatrâta with the compiler of the Udânavarga."[1] So likewise Tchandrakirti, cited by Burnouf,[2] mentions two Dharmatrâtas, a Sthavira and a Bhadanta, and it is highly probable, from Mr. Beal's catalogue of the Chinese Tripitaka, that both these Dharmatrâtas composed works. The Sthavira composed the Samyuktâbhidharma çastra (Catal. p. 82), but cannot have written the commentary on Aryadeva's Çataçastra Vaipulya,[3] for Aryadeva must have lived later than he.

The date of the first translation into Chinese of a collection of gâthâs by Dharmatrâta (A.D. 221–223), enables us, however, to limit the period in which the compiler of the Udânavarga can possibly have lived, and to assert that the work was composed somewhere between 75 B.C. and 200 A.D.

If we compare the Udânavarga with the Fa-kheu-pi-u,[4] it appears that in this latter work, out of 140 verses or parts of verses, there can be traced back to the Dhammapada about twenty-five which do not occur in the Tibetan version. This has led me to suppose that if the other works attributed to Dharmatrâta in the Chinese Tripitaka were examined, one might probably discover all the verses of the Dhammapada and quite a number of those of the Sutta Nipâta.

The Tibetan translation was made by Vidyaprabhâkara, who, from the fact that his name is frequently mentioned in connection with those of Çilendrabodhi, Dânaçila, &c.,

---

[1] See Târanâtha, p. 54, lig. 8.
[2] Burnouf, Intr. à l'Hist., p. 566.
[3] See Beal, Catalogue, pp. 76, 77, 82, and 108. In the Bstan-hgyur there are no works by Dharmatrâta except the present one.
[4] Beal, Texts from the Buddhist Canon, Trübner's Oriental Series.

well-known translators of the ninth century, was most likely in Tibet at about the same time, when King Ralpa-chan (A.D. 817-842) was giving great encouragement to translators of Buddhist works.

The commentary which has been made use of in the present work was composed by Pradjñavarman, who lived in Kachmere in the ninth century A.D.[1] Besides the present commentary entitled the Udânavarga vivarana, he composed a commentary on the Viceschastava by Siddhapati, and one on the Devâticayastotra by Sanskarapati. In the introduction to the Udânavarga vivarana[3] it is said that "Pradjñavarman was an Indian of Bhongala (Bhangala?), and a disciple of Bodhivarma of Kapadhyara (*sic*). He was born at Kava, in the country of Bhangala, and his fame was great; he was blessed with great steadfastness and sound understanding. Being blessed with the recollection of many of the flawless jewels uttered in the Dharma, he was of infinite service to the rest of mankind. His recollection of the many sayings of the holy law caused him to shine forth like the sun, and through the extent of his knowledge he dispelled the darkness that enveloped mankind, bringing them joy and confidence. . . . He composed, then, a commentary to help to set forth clearly the sayings which he used to speak to the multitudes. He kept the still beautiful cut flowers (of the Dharma) in their original form, but dispelled the obscurity of some of the utterances, making their perfections to burst forth like lotus flowers, and thus every one of the utterances of the most excellent of Munis (*i.e.*, Gautama) has become as bright as the sun. This commentary was therefore composed to extract the essence of the utterances of the Tathâgata, called 'words of great

---

[1] See Târanâtha, p. 204 trans.
[2] See Bstan-hgyur Stotra, Nos. 1 and 2, and Sûtra xxxiii., Nos. 100 and 101.
[3] Bstan-hgyur lxxi, fol. 54a, and vol. lxxii., fol. 244b. I find also mentioned in the Index of the Bst. a Pradjnavarma as a translator of Indian Buddhist works into Tibetan. It is most likely the same writer.

blessing,' or 'udânas'—fragments of the words of the Victorious One—and to teach their real signification."

This commentary is divided in thirty-three chapters, each one of which is devoted to a chapter of the text. Each verse is generally preceded by a short history of the events which caused the Buddha to speak it. In some cases these stories appear to have some historical value, but in the great majority they have evidently been invented to suit the text. In the Appendix there will be found a certain number of these "nidânas," as they are called by Pradjñâvarman, illustrating the different kinds of stories he joins to the text. In some few cases there is some analogy between the events related and those mentioned in Buddhaghosha's commentary on the Dhammapada, but it is unimportant.

The explanations of the words of each udâna are borrowed from the sûtras or the âgamas (*lung*); they are all of that literal description which one might expect of a "hinayanist" who did not pretend to extract from words anything more than their ordinary meaning. In the chapter on nirvâṇa he shows us that Tchandrakirti's observation about the Vaibâshika Dhamatrâta, that "he believed in the existence of things past and things future,"[1] is also applicable to him.

Let me here call attention to the use made throughout the Udânavarga of the word "nirvâṇa." In the greater number of cases it only implies the condition of Arhat, in which "sorrow has been left behind," "the nirvâṇa of the Arhat" (xxvi. 10), or in Pâli, *kilesanibbanam*. On the other hand, it cannot be understood to imply anything else but annihilation in such verses as xxvi. 27, in which it is defined as "not existence, not to be born." Here, then, it is in the "destruction of every particle of the elements of being (*skandhas*) or *anupâdisesanibbanam*."

It has frequently been asserted that the Northern Buddhist texts were of no value for a critical examination

---

[1] See Burnouf, *loc. cit.*, 566.

of early Buddhism; the Dhammapada was held up as being absolutely necessary for any correct understanding of the real ideas of Gautama.[1] I think, therefore, that when there exists so exact a rendering of every important verse of that book as is found in the present work, we are entitled to score a point in favour of the much-abused Tibetan and Chinese texts. It is a matter of deep regret to me that M. Schiefner, to whom we owe the first knowledge of the real contents of the Udânavarga, did not live to publish the translation of this work which he had undertaken, for in his hands it would have escaped much of the ill-treatment it has here experienced. However imperfect this translation may be, it is to be hoped that it will prove of some use, and that some indulgence will be shown to the translator of verses which are thus spoken of by the Chinese editor of the Fa-Kheu-king-tsu:[2] "The meaning of these gâthâs is sometimes very obscure, and men say that there is no meaning at all in them. But let them consider that it is difficult to meet with a teacher like Buddha, so the words of Buddha are naturally hard of explanation."

It remains for me to express my thanks to Dr. R. Rost, through whose kindness I have been able to avail myself of the rich collection of Tibetan works in the India Office, and also to Professor S. Beal, to whom I owe much valuable information concerning the Chinese version of the present work.

MONTREUX, *6th November* 1882.

---

[1] See for example Oldenburg's Buddha, sein Leben, &c., p. 198, where it is called "die schönste und reichste unter der Spruchsammlungen."

[2] Beal, Dhammapada, p. 30.

CONTENTS.

		PAGE
INTRODUCTION	. . .	vii

BOOK I.

CHAP.
I.	IMPERMANENCY	. . . .	1
II.	DESIRE	. . .	9
III.	LUST	. . . .	13
IV.	PURITY	. . . .	17
V.	AGREEABLE THINGS	. . .	24
VI.	MORALITY	. . . .	29
VII.	VIRTUOUS CONDUCT	. . . .	33
VIII.	SPEECH	. . . . .	36
IX.	DEEDS	. . . .	39
X.	FAITH	. . . .	43
XI.	THE ÇRAMANA	. . .	46
XII.	THE WAY	. . . .	49

BOOK II.

XIII.	HONOURS	. . .	57
XIV.	HATRED	. . . .	61
XV.	REFLECTION	. . . .	65
XVI.	MISCELLANEOUS	. . . .	70
XVII.	WATER	. . . . .	75

CONTENTS.

CHAP.		PAGE
XVIII.	THE FLOWER	78
XIX.	THE HORSE	83
XX.	ANGER	86
XXI.	THE TATHAGATA	90
XXII.	THE HEARER	94
XXIII.	SELF	98
XXIV.	NUMBERS	102

BOOK III.

XXV.	FRIENDSHIP	111
XXVI.	NIRVANA	116
XXVII.	SIGHT	125
XXVIII.	SIN	133
XXIX.	DAY AND NIGHT	141
XXX.	HAPPINESS	152

BOOK IV.

XXXI.	THE MIND	163
XXXII.	THE BHIXU	174
XXXIII.	THE BRAHMANA	185

APPENDIX	203
INDEX	217

UDÂNAVARGA.

(*In the Language of India,*[1] "*Udânavarga;*" *in the Language of Tibet,* "*Tched-du brjod pai tsoms.*")

Book I.

I.

IMPERMANENCY.

GLORY be to Him who knows all![2] Let there be happiness!

1.

The Victorious one[3] spoke these verses (udâna[4]); Hearken unto me while I tell them; what I say is to dispel sleep and torpor, and to bring gladness to the mind.

2.

The All-wise, the Protector, the Mighty one, the Very compassionate one, He who had finished with corporeal existence,[5] Bhagavat,[6] spoke (or has spoken) thus:

---

[1] The numbers in brackets refer to the verses of the Dhammapada. Notes followed by the letter P. (Pradjnâvarman) are translations from the Commentary.
[2] Sanskrit, Sarvadjna, epithet of the Buddha.
[3] Djina, epithet of the Buddha.
[4] The Commentary explains this word thus: "Udâna are sayings such as are found in this work."
[5] For the Sanskrit equivalents of all these names of the Buddha, see the Buddhist terminological dictionary, Mahâvyutpatti, chap. i.
[6] He is called Bhagavat, says P., because he has conquered pain, passions, hatred, ignorance, sin; for this is he "victorious." I was at first inclined to consider these two verses as an introduction, and to call No. 3 the first; but I have thought it best to adopt the commentator's arrangement. These verses, however, are not supposed to be udânas, but are by Dharmatrâta.

3.

Alas! the impermanency of created things (samkâra); what is created is subject to decay. As what has been born must come to destruction, happy they who are at rest![1]

4 (146).

To one who is being burnt,[2] what joy can there be, what subject of rejoicing? Ye who dwell in the midst of darkness,[3] why seek ye not a light?

5 (149).

Those pigeon-coloured bones[4] are thrown away and scattered in every direction; what pleasure is there in looking at them?

6.

One who has heretofore been subject to the misery[5] of birth from the womb may go to the highest place and come no more back again (into the world).

7.

One sees many men in the forenoon, some of whom one will not see in the afternoon; one sees many men in the afternoon, some of whom one will not see in the (next) forenoon.

8.

Many men and women do die even in their prime;

---

[1] Comp. Beal, Dhammapada, p. 32; Rhys-Davids, Parinibbanasutta, p. 117; Anityata Sutra (Mdo xxvi.), fol. 246a.

[2] "By the misery of sin and sorrow."—P.

[3] "The darkness of ignorance." The "light" implies faith, application, &c., says P.

[4] Comp. Vasubandhu gâthâsamgraha, 21; Mél. Asiat., viii. p. 565. "Pigeon - coloured," P. says, "is used to convey the idea of perishableness, for this pleasing colour fast fades away." Comp. the Pâli *kapoto*, "pigeon," and *kapotako*, "grey."

[5] I have tried to follow the suggestions of P. (fol. 746), but there are several words that embarrass me. The first two lines of this verse are: *gang-gi nub-mo kho-na-nas | mngal-du dang-por hjug-pai mi.* The verse was spoken to inspire confidence to the Bhixus, then at Çravasti, who thought that they would be subject to death (for ever?).

though men then be called young, what reliance can they place in life?

9.

Some die in the womb, some die at the birth,[1] some gradually decay, some pass away in the vigour of their manhood.

10.

Some are old, and some are young, some are grown up; by degrees they all do disappear, like ripe fruit falling.[2]

11.

As the ripe fruit is always filled with the dread of falling, so likewise he who has been born is filled with the fear of death.[3]

12.

It is with the life of mortal man as with the shining vases made from clay by the potter—they all finish by being destroyed.[4]

13 (347).

It is with the life of mortal man as with the spider, who, stretching hither and thither its web, is enclosed in it.

14.

It is with the life of mortal man as with (the spider), who, though it would free itself from its trap, finds, whichever way it takes a step, the abode of death before it.[5]

15.

As a river that is always running swiftly by and never returns are the days of man's life—they depart and come back no more.

---

[1] *Btsas-pai sar.* "The child dies after birth, while the mother is still in the house where she has been delivered." P. distinguishes four periods of life—(1.) in the womb, (2.) childhood, (3.) youth, (4.) manhood.

[2] Comp. Sallasutta (Sutta Nipâta), 5. [3] Comp. Sallasutta, 3.
[4] Comp. Burnouf, Lotus de la Bonne Loi, p. 86; and Sallasutta (Sutta Nipâta), 4.
[5] Comp. this and preceding verse with Beal, *loc. cit.*, p. 152.

16.

Joy[1] is fleeting and mixed with pain; it swiftly disappears, like figures traced on water with a wand.

17 (135).

As a cowherd with his staff gathers his cattle into the stable, so disease and old age bring mankind to the lord of death.[2]

18.

As the waters of a brook, so flow on by day and night the hours of man's life; it draws nearer and nearer to its end.

19 (60).

Long is the night to him who is watching, great the distance to him who is wayworn, and great the circle of transmigration to the fools who know not the holy Law.[3]

20 (62).

"These children are mine, these riches are mine;" with these (thoughts) is the fool disturbed. What are children and riches to one who (owns) not even himself in the other world?

21.

It is the law of humanity that, though one acquires hundreds and thousands of worldly goods, one still falls into the power of the lord of death.

22.[4]

The end of all that has been hoarded up is to be spent; the end of what has been lifted up is to be cast down; the end of meeting is separation; the end of life is death.

---

[1] Both the text of the Bkah-hgyur and that of the Bstan-hgyur read *dkah-ba*, "difficulty," which is evidently incorrect. The Commentary, fol. 836, has the correct reading, *dyah ba*.

[2] Comp. Beal, *loc. cit.*, p. 33.

[3] "The Four Truths."—P.

[4] Comp. Vasubandhu, *loc. cit.*, p. 569; Bkah-hgyur, i. 298, vii. 636; Schiefner, Tibet. Tales, p. 30; Beal, *loc. cit.*, p. 34.

23.

As the end of life is death, and all creatures do die, so likewise do virtue and vice bear fruits which follow after the deeds.

24 (126).

They who do evil go to hell;[1] they who are virtuous[2] go to happiness; they who have observed the right way and are without sin obtain nirvâṇa.[3]

25.

The Buddhas, the pratyeka Buddhas, and the disciples of the Buddhas cast off this body; what is the use of speaking of the ignorant crowd?[4]

26 (128).

There is no place where is not the pain of death, not in the sky nor in the midst of the sea, not even if one enters into the clefts of the mountains.

27.

All who have been and all who shall be, abandon this body and depart; the wise man who understands that (the body) is to be dreaded, lives a life of purity according to the Law.[5]

28.

Seeing old age, the pain of disease, and the death of the heedless, he who is earnest gives up a home that is like a prison;[6] but how can the common of mortals cast off desires?

---

[1] Comp. Beal, *loc. cit.*, p. 37, note 1.
[2] "He who has been charitable," &c.—P.
[3] "They will go to the city of nirvâṇa, which is the place where there is no remnant of the skandhas."—P.
[4] The Commentary omits this verse. The last line, *skye-bo phal-pa smos chi-dyos*, seems to imply that there is but little hope for the unbelievers who do not give up worldly passions.
[5] According to the text of the Bstan-hgyur, "abide in the Law and practise it," but the Commentary follows the text of the Bkah-hgyur.
[6] "Frees himself of humanity."—P.

29 (151).

Even the brilliant chariot of the king is destroyed, the body also draws nigh to old age; but the best of men,[1] who teaches others this best of all good laws, shall not know old age.

30.

Thou art foolish and despicable,[2] and doest not that which is right; for that body (rûpa) in which thou delightest will be the cause of thy ruin.

31.

One may live a hundred years, yet he is subject to the lord of death; one may reach old age, or else he is carried off by disease.[3]

32.

He[4] who is (always) changing without ceasing, decaying day and night, filled with the anguish of birth and death, is like the fish thrown in hot water.

33.

This life is fleeting away day and night; it is unstable like the stream of a great river; one goes on not to return again.[5]

34.

Man is like a fish in a shallow pool of water; day and night this life is passing away; what subject of rejoicing is there in so brief a thing?[6]

---

[1] "They who have become pure vessels and who are holy—*snod-du gyur tching skal-pa dang-ldan-pa dag-go.*"—P.
[2] *Ngan = smad.*—P.
[3] Comp. Sallasutta, 16.
[4] Bhagavat being on the shore of the stream that passed at Ayodyaya near the Ganges, saw some fishermen throw an old and decrepit fish into a pool of boiling water in the midst of the sands on the bank. The sight of the fish's convulsions and growing weakness suggested the simile. Pradj. fol. 94a.
[5] Comp. ver. 15.
[6] This verse is not in the Commentary. Comp. Beal, *loc. cit.*, p. 164.

35 (148).

The end of life is death; this body bent down by age, this receptacle of disease, is rapidly wasting away; this mass of corruption will soon be destroyed.

36 (41).

Alas! this body will soon lie on the earth unnoticed, empty,[1] senseless, thrown away in a cemetery like a billet of wood.[2]

37.

Continually afflicted by disease, always emitting some impurity, this body, undermined by age and death, what is the use of it?

38 (286).

"This (abode) will do for winter and (this) for summer;" thus ponders the rapidly decaying fool who has not seen the danger.[3]

39 (288).

Thou who art surrounded by children and flocks, children are no refuge, nor are father, mother, and kinsfolk; thou art without a refuge![4]

---

[1] *Stong-dsing*, "that is to say, without self (*bag-med*), separated from the three abodes (of the self), deprived of reason."

[2] Comp. Vijayasutta (Sutta Nipâta), 11, and Manava dharma çastra, iv. 241.

[3] According to the text of the Bstan-hgyur and to Pradj., this verse is as follows:—"Devote all the energy of this purulent body, which is rapidly decaying and subject to disease, to the acquisition of supreme peace. 'This will do for summer, this for the rainy season;' thus ponders the fool," &c. The first word of the fourth line seems to read *ñe*, but I can do nothing with it. I have substituted conjecturally *dsi*, "peace." This arrangement does not appear to me as good as that of the text of the Bkahhgyur that I have adopted. See Commentary, fol. 97b.

[4] Comp. Dhaniyasutta (Sutta Nipâta), 17, and Manava dharma çastra, iv. 239. According to Pradj., instead of this verse we ought to have two verses, which are:—

39.
"He who is surrounded by children and flocks,
Whose mind is distracted by passions,

40.

"Such and such actions are a source of felicity, which I, having performed them, will acquire." He who prepares himself in this manner will overcome age, disease, and death.

41.

Give yourselves up then to the unceasing joy of meditation (samâdhi); see the end of birth and age in the birth of diligence; overcome the hosts of Mâra and the Bhixus shall pass beyond birth and death.

Chapter on Impermanency, the First.

Is carried off by the lord of death,
As is a sleeping village by the flood.

40.

"When comes the hour of death,
There is no refuge for him in his children,
Nor are father, mother, or kinsfolk a refuge;
He is without a refuge!"

Comp. the first verse to xviii. 13.

II.

DESIRE (KÂMA).

1.

ALL indecision[1] produces desires; it is called the root of desire; suppress indecision and (desire) will arise in thee no more.

2 (215).[2]

From desires comes grief, from desires comes fear; he who is free from desires knows neither grief nor fear.

3 (214).

From pleasures comes grief, from pleasures comes fear; he who is free from pleasures knows neither grief nor fear.

4

The fruit of desires and pleasures ripens into sorrow; their at first agreeable fruit is burning, as the torch that has not been cast away does finally burn the fool.[3]

5 (345).

Look at those who are fondly attached to jewels, earrings, to their children (those are fetters); but iron, wood, and rope make not strong fetters, says the Blessed One.

---

[1] *Kun rtog*, which appears from fol. 230, vol. 71 of the Commentary to be equivalent to *rnam-rtog* (vikalpana).

[2] Comp. Beal, *loc. cit.*, p. 119.

[3] Comp. Sutra in forty-two sections, sect. xxiv.

6 (346).

It is hard for one who is held by the fetters of desire to free himself of them, says the Blessed One. The steadfast, who care not for the happiness of desires, cast them off, and do soon depart (to nirvâna).

7.

There is no being in the world who is not through his indecision affected by desires, yet they who are steadfast seek to free themselves of desires, though they do pervade the world.[1]

8.

Mankind has no lasting desires; they are impermanent in them who experience them: free yourselves then from what cannot last, and abide not in the sojourn of death.[2]

9.

The sinless and reflective mind in which a desire arises experiences no misery[3] from it; the different desires disturb it not: he who (has such a mind) is beyond death, I declare.

10 (239).

As the smith does with the silver, so does the intelligent man, gradually and little by little, cleanse himself of all his impurities.[4]

11.

As the shoemaker, when he has well prepared his

---

[1] This verse is very obscure, and I offer my translation with great diffidence.

[2] "Spoken to convince of error a parivrâdjaka, who, among other arguments, said it is not necessary for three reasons to cast off desires. 1. If they are permanent, they are a treasure (gter). 2. If they are not permanent, they are like the horn of a hare (nonentities, nonsense). 3. If they are not injurious, they are like the aryamarga." See Commentary, fol. 109a.

[3] "Misery (zag-pa), it is called thus because it drops (zag) from out the different regions of the six ayatanas as drops (hdzag) water through holes." Comp. the Sanskrit asrava, meaning also "oozing out, misery."

[4] Comp. Sutra in 42 sections, sect. xxxiv.

DESIRE.

leather, can use it to make shoes, so when one has cast off desires, he has the highest happiness.

12.

If one longs for happiness, let him cast off all desires; he who has cast off all desires will find the most perfect happiness.

13.

As long as one follows after desire, one finds no satisfaction; they who through wisdom have given it up find contentment.

14.

Desires are never satiated; wisdom affords contentment: he who has the contentment of wisdom cannot fall into the power of lust.

15.

They who have fondness for pleasure, and who delight only in what is wrong,[1] would not perceive the danger they run, even if their life were drawing to a close.

16.

The evil-minded is subdued by wealth and seeks not after the other world; his mind is subverted by his fondness for desires; he brings destruction on himself and on others.

17 (186).

Even a shower of Karçapanas[2] would not satisfy the covetous; the wise know full well that desires bring little contentment and (much) pain.

---

[1] The text is: *de-dag kye-ma tchos min tchos.* I have tried to follow the suggestions of the Commentary. The correct reading is probably *de-dag-kyi ma-tchos,* &c.

[2] "A weight of gold or silver equal to sixteen marshas."—Wilson, Sans. Dict., p. 199. P. says, "There are a diversity of Karçapanas, some made of gold, &c. Others say that the copper pana piece (*zangs-mai pa-nai tchad*) is called Karçaka."

18 (187).

Not even in the pleasures of the gods does the disciple of the perfect Buddha find pleasure; he rejoices only in the destruction of desires.

19.

Even[1] a mountain of riches like unto Himavat would not suffice for the wealth of a single man; he who has understanding knows this full well.

20.

They[2] who know that this (*i.e.*, desire) is the origin of sorrow, how can they delight in pleasures? Having learnt that this is the cause of pain in the world, they acquire steadfastness to help to control themselves.

Chapter on Desire, the Second.

---

[1] "Spoken by Bhagavat while residing in a large town (*grong-brdal*) of the Çakyas, called Çilavati."—P. fol. 109b. Comp. Beal, *loc. cit.*, p. 108.

[2] These last four verses are in Mr. Ralston's English translation of M. Schiefner's miscellaneous writings. The last verse he translates thus: "He who observes sorrow starting from this base, how can he take pleasure in enjoyments? He who is steady, who has learnt to recognise the thorn in the treasures of the world, will learn the essence of things to his own correction." See Tibetan Tales, p. 19.

III.

LUST (TRICHNÂ).

1.

MANKIND is subdued by its indecision;[1] he who considers evil passions as pure, increases and multiplies his passions and adds to the strength of his bonds.

2.

He who continually keeps present in his mind that the quieting of indecision is peace, and that it is not agreeable, frees himself from all lust and destroys his bonds.

3.

Desires envelop one as it were in darkness; one is torn to pieces by delighting in lust; the heedless are held fast by their bonds, as are fish to their watery homes.[2]

4 (284).

Beings who give themselves up to their heedlessness, their lustfulness increases as does a creeper;[3] they run after old age and death as does the calf after its mother when longing for milk.

---

[1] Comp. note to verse 1, ch. ii.

[2] The last line of this gâtha is *tsed mar tchud-bai ña dang hdra*. *Tsed* I have translated as equivalent to *htso-ba*, "to live." The comment is so much effaced here that I have not been able to make use of it.

[3] "Or more correctly called *maluta*," the Commentary says.

5 (334).

He whose mind is impure and who is passionate, and who seeks after happiness, runs hither and thither in the orb (of birth), like the monkey in the forest seeking for fruit.

6 (342).

Continually longing for happiness and walking in the way of birth and death, mankind is led on by its passions, and runs about like a hare in a net.[1]

7.

They who are held in the folds of lustfulness, who care only for what concerns existence (lit. existence and not existence), the fools delighting only in the enjoyments of attachment (yoga),[2] will find suffering again and again.

8.

Beings who are without righteousness (correct religious views) and peace of mind, who have all the attachments of Mâra (sinful attachments), run after old age and death as does the calf after its mother when longing for milk.

9.

He who casts off lust and the like, who is without affection for what is or is not existence, the Bhixu,[3] has conquered existence and will attain the perfect and unsurpassable nirvâṇa.

---

[1] According to the version of the Bst., there ought to be six lines to this verse, the two extra ones being placed after the second line. The verse would be as follows: "Continually longing for happiness and walking in the way of birth and death, one is held by the bonds of Mâra and is walking in the way of old age and death; mankind is led on by its fancies," &c. Again, the comment reads, instead of "bonds of Mâra," "delighting in the enjoyment of every (form) of attachment (yoga)," as in next verse.

[2] "The four yogas or attachments are—attachment to sensual pleasure, to existence, to false doctrine, to ignorance." See Childers, s.v. "Yogo."

[3] "Bhixu" here, and very generally throughout this work, implies, not a Buddhist mendicant, but "one who has overcome all evil influences." Nirvâṇa here means the nirvâṇa not having any particle of the skandhas remaining; in Pâli, *anupâdiscsanibbânam*.

10 (335).

He who has cast off the world, which is hard to do, must become insensible to love for women (or women's love), for it increases sorrow as does a shower the (birana) grass.

11 (336).

He who has cast off the world, which is hard to do, and has become insensible to love for women, sorrow falls from off him as does the water drop from the lotus.[1]

12 (337, 1st part).

Therefore as many as are here come together; this salutary word I tell unto you: Pull up the weed of lust by the root as one does the (birana) grass for the sake of the uçira (root).[2]

13 (337, 2nd part).

They who are given to the company of lustfulness wander about for a long time; so pull up lust by the root, and sorrow and fear are no more.

14 (341).

Again and again seeking for it (existence), they again and again enter the womb; beings come and go; to one state of being succeeds another.

15.

It is hard to cast off (existence) in this world; he who has cast off lust, who has pulled up the seed (of existence), will no more be subject to transmigration, for he has put an end to lust.

16.

Care not about abiding in the conditions of humanity,[3]

---

[1] Comp. Bhagavad gitâ, v. 10.
[2] Uçira is the name given to the root of the birana grass.—P.
[3] Dal-hbyor, which the comment explains as being the mi-khom-pa brgyad. M. Jäschke says this latter expression means "the eight obstacles of happiness, caused by the re-birth

which hold one captive among gods and men, but cross over from the regions of lust. If one is born in hell, the human condition (*dal-hbyor*) is at an end, and one repents him (of his mistake).

17 (340).

The channels of lust are the source (of transmigration). Lust in (this) world is the root of the vine, which creeps up and entwines one as in the folds of a net. If one does not destroy this tormentor, he will be subject to ever-recurring suffering, and will never leave it entirely behind.

18 (338).

As long as a live tree has not been pulled up by the roots, but only cut down, it springs up afresh; so it is that if even the smallest atom of lust has not been eradicated, one will not leave behind this ever-recurring suffering (*i.e.*, existence).

19.

As he who has himself made a weapon is killed by it when in the robber's hands, so likewise the being in whose heart lust has arisen will be killed by it.

20.

Knowing then the sufferings that come from lust and its punishment,[1] having cast off lust, without eagerness for anything, the reflective Bhixu has departed entirely (from this world).[2]

Chapter on Lust, the Third.

---

in places or situations unfavourable to conversion." *Dal-hbyor* also, according to M. Jäschke, is "often used directly for condition of humanity, or of human nature." This verse is rather obscure.

[1] There are two punishments (*ñes-dmigs*), the principal of which is transmigration.—P.

[2] *Kun-tu rgyus*, generally used to render the Sanskrit parivrâdjaka, but here, according to the comment, it means, "he will obtain the anupâdisesanibbâna."

IV.

PURITY.

1 (21).

THE pure man knows not death; he who is impure dwells with death; he who is pure will not die;[1] he who is impure dies repeatedly.

2 (22).

The wise who know this difference delight in modesty and purity; their pleasure is that of the elect.[2]

3 (23).

With this (idea) incessantly present to their minds, and always firm in their resolution to gain the other side, they (finally) enjoy nirvâṇa,[3] that unsurpassable felicity.

4 (28).

When the wise men through earnestness[4] have overcome heedlessness, then, steadfast through wisdom, they ascend to above the abode of the gods, and, free from sorrow and pain, they look down as from the summit of a mountain at the fools[5] on the face of the earth.[6]

---

[1] "For he has attained nirvâṇa."—P.

[2] "Province of activity of the elect. Bhagavat has said that the four smriti upasthâna were the field of activity of the elect."—P.

[3] "They put an end to misery."—P.

[4] *Bag-yod* = *apramada*. P. says "it is a mind which, proof against every sorrow (asrava), holds fast to the laws of virtue." It admits, as also *bag-med* = *pramada*, of many translations. The Commentary adds, "Such as Çariputra were *bag-yod*; some of the (ordinary) priests and laymen are *bag-med*."

[5] "He who suffers from sorrow."—P.

[6] Compare Mahâvagga i. 5, 7.

5 (25).

The[1] wise man through earnestness, virtue, and purity makes himself an island which no flood can submerge.

6.

'Tis the earnest that become far-famed by their diligence, reflection, the purity of their lives, their judgment, their perfect observance (of the commandments), by their whole life which is according to the law.

7.

One must apply oneself to acquire superior insight and the foundation of the condition of the Muni. He who is wrapped up in his uninterrupted thoughts of peace knows no sorrow (nibbuta).[2]

8.

Have nothing to do with false doctrines, have nothing to do with the heedless; he who delights not in false theories shall not continue (in) the world.[3]

9.

He who has correct ideas of the world shall acquire such greatness, that though he goes through a thousand regenerations, he shall not fall into the evil way.

10.

The (mind of the) fool who is given up to carelessness

---

[1] "Spoken in answer to a question of Asivangaka, the son of a merchant."—P. The wise man "is one who has perceived the four truths."—P.

[2] See Pratimoxa Sûtra, and Mél. Asiat., viii. pp. 591 and 593. The commentator does not analyse this verse here; he places it after ver. 9.

[3] *Hjig-rten hphel-bar mi byao.* P. condemns the way I have translated, and says this expression "does not mean to escape from the circle of transmigration, but to acquire perfect understanding." I have, however, followed the text as exactly as possible.

PURITY.

is perverted;[1] the wise man must be careful, as is the head of a caravan watching his treasures.

11.

He who is not given up to carelessness, who finds no delight in pleasures, whose mind is always attentive, will put an end to sorrow.[2]

12.

He[3] who has put an end to sorrow, and is not given to carelessness in this world, can no more be hurt by the careless than can the lion by the antelope.

13 (309).

The shameless man[4] who covets his neighbour's wife will experience these four conditions: he acquires (bad) reputation, troubled sleep, thirdly scorn, and fourthly he goes to hell.

14 (310).

He who, acting not virtuously, doeth evil, indulges but for a moment, amidst fear and trembling, his burning passion, and then he has to bear the heavy punishment of the king, and he is burnt in hell.

15.

He who seeks after happiness, let him act vigorously;[5] the steadfast makes no slothful exertions like those of the foolish waggoners.

---

[1] *Bsam-brlag*, "whose ideas are irrational, or, as others explain it, one who, careless through ignorance, listens not to the law."—P.

[2] "Will be freed from the three kinds of misery (kleça)."—P.

[3] There are several words in this verse which are evidently corrupt, but as I do not find them in the Commentary, I am unable to correct the text. P. gives several explanations of the simile.

[4] *Bag-med mi* = Pâli *naro pamatto*, "his neighbour's wife," *pharol bud med*. Comp. Pâli *paradâro*.

[5] *Gong-ma bdsin-du bya*. This translation is not very exact, but I think that it conveys the sense of the original. "Bhagavat was residing in the Anarjana grove (*sic*, *i.e.*, Añjanavana) of Sâketa, and had gone with a great number of Bhixus into the town of Sâketa to collect

16.

When the fools with their waggons have given up the highroad and have entered a bad road, they deeply grieve over their mistake.[1]

17.

In like manner, the fool who gives up the law and follows that which is not the law falls into the power of the lord of death; he also is destroyed by reason of his want of sight.

18.

They who do not what ought to be done, and who do that which ought not to be done, who glory in their carelessness, increase the extent of their troubles, and he who adds to his misery finds its cessation a long way off.[2]

19.

He who comprehends the nature of the body, who reflects, and whose exertions are unceasing, does not what ought not to be done, and does what ought to be done.

20.

He, therefore, with memory and understanding will put an end to his misery, and when he has put an end to his misery (asrava), he will find the untroubled state.[3]

21.

As many as you be, I declare unto you that those who, though they have heard but little of the law, have followed

---

[1] alms. It happened that some waggons having given up the highway, had taken to a cross road, in which the axles broke down. (The owners) then saw that they ought to have remained in the highway they had left. Bhagavat, who had been witness of the occurrence, spoke these three verses (15-17) to illustrate this event."—P. fol. 151a.

[1] *Mig tchag*, "at the time of death the eye and the other organs gradually give way."—P. These words occur at the end of ver. 17.

[2] "Nirvâṇa is afar off."—P.

[3] The Commentary makes one verse out of 19 and 20.

22 (19).

Even if the careless man can recite a large portion (of the law), he follows it not; he is like a cowherd counting the cattle of others; he has no share in the priesthood.[1]

23 (20).

He who, though he can only recite a few lines (of the law), walks in the path of the law, and has forsaken passion, anger, and ignorance, he has a share in the priesthood.

24.

He whose speech exalts earnestness and who always despises heedlessness will be greater among the gods than he who has made a hundred sacrifices.

25.

The sage who praises earnestness in his speech knows what is right and what is wrong; the sage holds fast to earnestness for two reasons: for the blessings it brings this life, and also on account of the future; the steadfast who have understood this are called sages.

26 (327).

The Bhixu[2] who delights in purity and who looks with dread on impurity will pull himself from out the evil way as the elephant pulls himself from out the mire.

27.

The Bhixu who delights in purity and who looks with dread on impurity shakes off sin as does the wind the leaves of a tree.

---

[1] See Commentary, fol. 155b. Comp. this verse and preceding one with Sûtra in 42 sections, xxxviii.

[2] According to P., the five verses (26-30) were spoken on the same occasion. The Commentary says six, which includes the one mentioned, p. 22 note 1. Compare Sûtra in 42 sections, xli.

28.

The Bhixu[1] who delights in purity and who looks with dread on impurity puts an end to all attachments and gradually arrives at felicity.

29.

The Bhixu who delights in purity and who looks with dread on impurity arrives at perfect comprehension of rest from the sanskâra, the perfection of peace.[2]

30.

The Bhixu who delights in purity and who looks with dread on impurity is so near nirvâṇa[3] that he cannot fail (to reach it).

31.

The diligent and virtuous man, who lives according to the law,[4] finds by following the law happiness in this world and in the other.[5]

32.

Ye who are earnest in learning for the sake of rest (nirvâṇa), exerting yourselves and filled with application, consider well the lives of those unreflecting, careless, negligent, uncontrolled, and lazy men who have turned away from learning, and hearken not to the unreflecting.

33.

The Bhixu who is truly moral[6] and who delights in

---

[1] The Commentary and the text of the Bst. insert before this verse one which ends by these two lines: "He casts off all attachments, and they vanish as if burnt up by fire." The first line is completely effaced in the text, and the comment does not give it in full. See Commentary 7, fol. 159a. Cf. Dham. 31.

[2] Dsi-bai-yo-hphang, in Pâli amatam padam, seems to correspond with this expression.

[3] "To escape the circle of transmigration."—P. Or we may translate it, "he cannot possibly fall away from it."

[4] "Who is virtuous in body, speech, and mind."—P.

[5] Pha-rol, "other side." Here, we are told it means "in other births."

[6] Tsul-khrims = çila. See Spence Hardy, Manual of Buddhism, p. 506 et seq. "Bhixu implies one who can and does keep the moral precepts."—P.

PURITY.

earnestness brings thus all his thoughts well under control, and his mind is in safety.

34.

Arise, commence a new life, turn towards the doctrine of the Buddha; trample down the hosts of the lord of death as an elephant does a house of mud.[1]

35.

Whoever has lived according to this law of discipline, in gentleness and purity, will, having cast off transmigration, put an end to his misery.[2]

Chapter on Purity, the Fourth.

---

[1] Comp. Pratimoxa Sûtra, Dulva v. fol. 30; Burnouf, Intr. à l'Hist. du Buddh., pp. 184 and 342, where it occurs in the Prâtiharya Sutra. P. imagines a special event for this verse; see fol. 163a.

[2] Comp. Pratimoxa, where the text is slightly different; Burnouf, *loc. cit.*, pp. 184 and 342; also Bhixuni vinaya vibhanga, fol. 483.

V.

AGREEABLE THINGS.

1 (212).

From those things that are agreeable comes sorrow; from those things that are agreeable comes fear: if one casts off agreeable things he will be without sorrow, without fear.

2.

From that which is enjoyable[1] comes fear; from the agreeable comes misery, from the agreeable fear: if that which is pretty changes, one reaps but despair.

3.

The miseries[2] of the world are numerous — sorrow, lamentations, cries, &c.; they all arise from holding on to those things that are agreeable: if one gives up what is agreeable they will all cease to be.

4.

They for whom there is nothing whatever agreeable in the world are happy and without sorrow; they therefore who would be without affliction, free from human passions,[3] must never do that which is agreeable.

---

[1] *Sdug-gu-ma.* This verse is intended to teach "that he who would cast off all that is harmful must free himself from all that has the appearance of being agreeable."—P. 165b.

[2] The six verses that follow were spoken on the same occasion.

[3] *Rdul,* "dust," copied in the Sanskrit *raya,* and here used for "evil desire, passion," &c., as in the original.

5 (210).

Not to see what is agreeable is painful, so likewise is the sight of what is not agreeable; one must never seek what is agreeable; he must not seek what is not agreeable.

6.

It is by being deprived of what is agreeable and by finding what is disagreeable that men create (for themselves) the intolerable sorrow of age.

7.

When that in which one delights does die, such as one's kinsfolk or friends, it brings one a great and enduring sorrow, for to be separated from that which brings pleasure is painful.

8.

He who knows neither agreeable or disagreeable is without bonds; he, therefore, who considers the agreeable as sinful will give up what is agreeable.

9.

He who, having ceased to consider what is agreeable, has nought to do with attachment to (worldly) happiness, who has attachment to the happiness that is not that of the individual, seeks the object of his fond desires (nirvâṇa).[1]

10.

He who among gods and men is held by fondness for what is pleasing in the body (rûpa), does evil and suffers affliction, he falls into the power of age and death.

---

[1] This verse is one of the most difficult to translate in this work. The comment substantially says, "They who comprehend the agreeable, who have learnt what is evil and have renounced it, who have given up what profits only their being, strive to enjoy the object of their desires, which is the *bslab-pa-gsum* or three perfections (?)." See Jäschke, s.v. "Bslab."

11.

He who is steadfast both by day and night, who casts away what is pleasing in the body (rûpa), which is difficult to do, pulls up by the very roots sin, that food of Mâra.

12.

The foolish people,[1] who consider what is not good as good, what is not agreeable as agreeable, what is misery as happiness, will surely come to destruction.[2]

13.

He who, doing evil, would be made happy by it, finds no contentment, let him not do evil.[3]

14.

He who, doing what is right, would be made happy by it, finds contentment, let him not do evil.

15.

As the frontier town is protected by strong retrenchments, so let him who would be happy protect himself by strong defences.

16 (157).

The wise man who would be made happy watches during all the three watches;[4] his watchfulness makes him safe.

17 (315).

When the frontier town is well guarded within and

---

[1] Spoken by Bhagavat while residing in the Amalakalava (Amalakavana?) of a Çakya village, because he would not rejoice at the birth of a child.

[2] Verses 13-17 were spoken for the edification of Prasenajit, king of Kosala, who, at that time living in solitude, was thinking of what might be of pleasure to one's self. Bhagavat explained that when the body and mind were rightly employed one enjoyed real pleasure.

[3] The text of the Bk. reads *sdug*, "agreeable," but the Commentary reads *sdig*, and we find this reading in the next verse.

[4] *Thun*, lit. "night watches." See fol. 172. Compare Sûtra in 42 sections, xlii.: "To the Tathâgata the research for nirvâna is like watching day and night."

without, its peace is not disturbed:[1] do likewise and watch thyself; for when one has been born in hell his peace is gone and he repents him (of what he has left undone).

18.

Look where you will, there is nothing dearer to man than himself; therefore, as it is the same thing that is dear to you and to others, hurt not others with what pains yourself.[2]

20 (130).

To all men this life is dear; all men fear punishment; you, who are like unto them, strike not, put not to death.

21 (219).

He who has been to a great distance and who returns from afar without mishap, his assembled kinsfolk and friends receive him with joyful cries of "Alala!"[3]

22 (220).

So likewise he who has been virtuous,[4] on arriving from this world into another, his good works receive him like kinsfolk and welcome him.

23.

Lay up, therefore, good works in view of the other world; for it is good works that receive beings in the other world.

24.

He whose life is one of virtue is praised by the gods; he in whom there is nothing to be blamed finds perfect joy in heaven.

---

[1] *Mi thal-pa.* The text of the Bk. reads *mi thos-pa*, but the comment apparently follows this reading; the leaf which refers to this verse, however, is very much effaced.

[2] Comp. Bst. cxxiii. fol. 174; Csoma, Tib. Gram. p. 167; also Hitopadesa, i. çl. 11.

[3] Used to express joy or astonishment, like *e-ma*, "well done!"

[4] *Bsod-nams byas,* "who has done good works, who has been charitable," &c.— P. Comp. with this verse, Manava dharma çastra, iv. 242.

25.

He who observes the law, who is perfectly virtuous, modest, speaking the truth, doing what he ought to do, delights the rest of mankind.

26.

He who, doing what he ought to do, and who, extolling the true law, gives to others pleasure, shall find joy in the other world.

27.

His speech is edifying, and he has given up all wrong doings, in this delights the righteous, and delights not the unrighteous.

28.

Therefore what is good and what is not good are separated at death; the unrighteous go to hell, the righteous go to heaven.[1]

Chapter on Pleasure, the Fifth.

---

[1] *Mtho-ris*, "heaven," "that is to say, the abode of the gods."—P. It corresponds to the expression, which occurs elsewhere, of "they obtain happiness."

VI.

MORALITY (ÇÎLA).

1.

The sage, for the sake of acquiring the three kinds of happiness, praiseworthiness, treasures,[1] and to go to the abode of happiness in the other world, watches well his conduct.[2]

2.

The sage, besides these objects, watches well his conduct for the sake of acquiring saintliness, most perfect sight,[3] and worldly peace.[4]

3.

Morality brings happiness; the body is free from pain; at night one's rest is peaceful, and on awakening one is still happy.

4.

The wise, who are charitable, and who observe the (other) moral precepts, acquire by the merit of charity endless happiness in this world and in the other.

---

[1] *Nor*, "to obtain everything that can be wished for by human and superhuman beings. "As, for example, the advent of a Buddha."—P.

[2] *Tsul-khrims* = *çila*, but here corresponding with *legs-par spyod*, "good conduct, a righteous life."

"The body and mind are cool like water, tchandana wood, &c."—P.

[3] "The eye of truth."—P. Sansk. *vipaçyanâ*.

[4] *Hjig-rten dsi ra*, "to be free of the three regions of human passions, to pass away from the grief of the road of ignorance."—P.

5.

It is well for him who observes, even unto old age, morality and virtue, and who is a believer: wisdom is the greatest treasure of man; 'twould be hard indeed for a robber to steal away the merit (of one's good works).

6–7.

The Bhixu who observes the moral laws,[1] whose senses are controlled, who is sober in his food, who gives not himself up to sleep; he who is thus diligent, who is never lazy day and night, is so near nirvâṇa that he cannot possibly fail (to reach it).

8.

Observing the moral laws, his mind and understanding[2] diligent in meditation, by such a life will the Bhixu[3] arrive at the destruction of misery.

9.

He consequently who is careful to observe the moral laws and meditation will acquire supernatural sight and discriminate according to knowledge.

10.

Then he will, having destroyed all his attachments,[4] enfranchised his mind, be separated from all things, and, possessed of knowledge, he goes beyond an incalculable quantity of sorrows.[5]

---

[1] "The Pratimoxa."—P.

[2] *Sems dang ye-shes*, i.e., "acquiring meditation and wisdom, they destroy kleça by this means as with a thunderbolt (vadjra)."—P.

[3] "One who, having put an end to every particle of kleça, attains in the heavens (*dyings*) parinirvâṇa."—P.

[4] *K'un-sbyor*, i.e., "put an end to the whole body of passions."—P.

[5] *Byrang-du-med-pai mya-nyan-hdas.* "I do not say that these perfect Bhixus go to the western region (Sukhavati). Happiness of nirvâṇa is here used to imply that one attains the longed-for goal."—P.

MORALITY.

11.

He who devotes himself to these three things, morality, meditation, and knowledge, arrives finally at perfect purity, and puts an end to pain and also to existence.

12.

He who is released from the bonds of the passions, who has cast away the body and who has wisdom,[1] has passed beyond the kingdom of Mâra,[2] and shines in splendour as does the sun.

13.

A Bhixu who outwardly and inwardly is impure and arrogant will not arrive at the perfection of morality, meditation, and wisdom.

14.

The rain falls from a sky covered by clouds, it falls not from a clear sky; remove then that which obscures (the mind)[3] and the rain will not fall.

15.

He who always sees and keeps the moral laws of the Bhixu[4] does speedily arrive on the road to nirvâṇa at perfect purity.

16 (54).

The odour of the flower travels not against the wind, nor does that of aloe-wood,[5] of incense, or of tchandana. The odour of the holy travels even against the wind; all regions are pervaded by the fragrance of the perfect man.

---

[1] "The knowledge of the cessation and of the non-production (of sorrow.)"—P.

[2] The lord of death.—P.

[3] The darkness of ignorance obscures the view of the four truths.—P.

[4] The rules of the Vinaya.—P.

[5] *Rtsa-ba*, lit. "root," but the Commentary explains it by "agaru and such like." Jäschke explains this word by "aloe-wood, agallochum, calambac."

17 (55).

Incense, tchandana, utpala, and mallika,[1] among these sweet perfumes the sweet odour of morality (or virtue) is unsurpassed.

18 (56).

How mean is the sweet odour that comes from incense (tagara) and tchandana; the sweet odour of those who possess morality penetrates even heaven.

19 (57).

They therefore who live in thoughtfulness, who are perfectly purified by their moral conduct, and who are emancipated by the perfectness of their knowledge,[2] will not meet with the road of Mâra.

20.

This[3] is the road that leads to happiness; he who has entered on this road of perfect purity will by keeping to it cast off the bonds of Mâra.[4]

Chapter on Morality, the Sixth.

---

[1] *Malika*, in the text, or jasmine. See Childers' Pâli Dict. s.v. "Malika is a flower."—P.

[2] Who are free from the kleça of the three regions (of desire).—P.

[3] Morality, earnestness, &c.—P.

[4] The snares of Mâra, such as being subject to death, affliction, slothfulness, &c.—P.

VII.

VIRTUOUS CONDUCT.[1]

1.

He who casts away wickedness in the body for a virtuous bodily course of life will be secure in his body if he is guarded against the great sins of the body.

2.

He who casts away wickedness in speech for virtuous speech will be secure in his speech if he is guarded against the great sins of speech.

3.

He who has cast away wickedness in thought for virtuous thoughts will be secure in his thoughts if he is guarded against the great sins of thought.

4.

He who has cast away wickedness in the body, who has cast away wickedness in speech, who has cast away wickedness in (his) thoughts, has cast away likewise all other stains.

5.

He who does what is virtuous in the body, he who is virtuous in his speech, he who is virtuous in his thoughts, will possess the four immeasurables.[2]

---

[1] In the Chinese version the title of this chapter is "Intelligence."

[2] *Tsad-med bdsi,* "the four immeasurable (merits)."

6.

He who is virtuous in body, speech, and mind, obtains unceasing happiness here and in the other world.

7.

The sage whose body is well controlled[1] can be harmed by nothing; he goes to an immortal dwelling-place, where there is no sorrow.

8.

The sage whose speech is well controlled can be harmed by nothing; he goes to an immortal dwelling-place, where there is no sorrow.

9.

The sage whose thoughts are always controlled can be harmed by nothing; he goes to an immortal dwelling-place, where there is no sorrow.

10.

The steadfast control their bodies, the steadfast control their speech, the steadfast control their minds; when the steadfast are well controlled in everything, they go to an immortal dwelling-place, where there is no sorrow.

11.

It is good to control the body, it is good to control the tongue (speech), it is good to control the mind; to have everything controlled is good: the Bhixu who is entirely controlled is freed from all sorrows.[2]

12.

Watching over his speech, his mind well controlled,

---

[1] Who carefully observes the rules of the Pratimoxa.—P.

[2] See Pratimoxa Sûtra, 9; Mel. Asiat., viii. pp. 591, 592.

doing nothing that is evil with his body, by observing these three ways of doing one finds the way spoken of by the Rischi.[1]

Chapter on Virtuous Conduct, the Seventh.

---

[1] Gautama is frequently called the Great Rischi (Mahârischi). Comp. Pratimoxa Sûtra, 10, *loc. cit*, p. 592.

VIII.

SPEECH.

1 (306).

He who says he has not done that which he has done, and he who is a liar, will go to hell; both these men alike, having gone to the next world, will be in a degraded state.

2.

Every man that is born, and who speaks wicked words, will cut himself with the axe of speech that has been born (with him).[1]

3.

He who praises a man who ought to be blamed, and who blames a man worthy of praise, brings sin[2] (upon himself) with his mouth; he who is sinful will not find happiness.[3]

4.

He who in this world loses his wealth at dice is a

---

[1] Comp. Sutta Nipâta, 657 (Kokâliyasutta, 1). Pradj. Comm. agrees with the Sutta Nipâta as to the origin of these four verses. The calumniator is called Kokâlika, a Bhixu who, having accepted the false theories of Devadatta, was residing with him in the Venuvana. He uses the same terms to describe the progress of Kokâliya's malady: "the boils, from being as large as mustard seeds, became as large as lentils (sran-ma)," &c. Cf. Manu, iv. 256.

[2] *Ithab-khrol*. Jäschke, "dispute, contest;" but P. says, "Some persons understand by *hthab-khrol* to do injury; but this is not exact, as it means that they do themselves such injury that it will prevent them enjoying (happiness)."

[3] Comp. Kokâliyasutta, 2.

little sinful;[1] he whose mind is evilly disposed towards the Tathâgata is an extremely sinful person.[2]

5.

He who in this world uses his speech and mind in reviling an Ariya will go for ten millions (of lives) to the Nirabbudas[3] hell, and for a thousand and forty-one to the Abbudas.[4]

6.

He who in the sinfulness of his mind accuses one who is not sinful of guilt, increases his own punishment in hell. He who has the might (of wisdom) makes no wrong use of his speech; not even in his mind does he imagine strife.

7 (164).

They whose minds are perverted by false doctrines (heresies), and who renounce the teaching and the mode of living of the elect (Ariyas) and Arhats, are destroyed on account of their wicked deeds as is the reed by its seed.[5]

8.

One must only speak what is right, and must not speak evilly; from wicked words comes evil,[6] one ought consequently to use proper language.

9.

The fool speaks wickedly, and it is by his speech that he is held in bondage; when one uses this kind of language and rejects the other,[7] him I call not a sage.

---

[1] Hthab-khrol.
[2] Comp. Kokâliyasutta, 3.
[3] The Comm. gives the same description of the length of a life in these hells as does the Sutta Nipâta, pp. 120, 121. Ud, vir., vol. 71, fol. 193.
[4] Comp. Kokâliyasutta, 4.
[5] Spoken on account of Dêvadatta's five propositions to reform the life of the Bhixus. See Appendix.
[6] Not to others, but to the speaker.—P.
[7] According to the Commentary, "other" refers to the other world.

10.

The Bhixus, who watch over their speech, who speak leisurely and without arrogance, who, in possession of the Law, do teach its value, their speech is pleasing.

11.

Well-spoken language is the principal thing, says the Ariya; to speak kindly and not unkindly is the second (best thing); to speak the truth and not lies is the third; to speak what is right and not what is futile is the fourth.[1]

12.

He who speaks words which bring him no grief and which will do no harm to his neighbour, speaks well.[2]

13.

Let one speak pleasing words, which, when he has spoken them, bring joy to his neighbour, and, being received with pleasure, cause him to commit no sin.[3]

14.

To speak the truth is (like) amrita; truth cannot be surpassed. The truth is holding fast to what is good and to what is right, say the righteous.[4]

15.

The words which the Buddha speaks and which remove all misery are words of truth; those that lead to nirvâna cannot be surpassed.[5]

Chapter on Speech, the Eighth.

---

[1] Comp. Subhâsittasutta, 1 (Sutta Nipâta, 449).
[2] Comp. Sutta Nipâta, 450 (Subhâsitasutta, 2).
[3] Comp. Subhâsitasutta, 3.
[4] Comp. Subhâsitasutta, 4.
[5] Comp. Subhâsitasutta, 5.

IX.

DEEDS.

1 (176).

The man who gives up the one (great) law (*i.e.*, truth), the means of gaining (happiness in) the other world, and who speaks lies, there is no evil that he will not do.[1]

2 (308).

Better it would be that a man should eat a lump of flaming iron than that one who is unrestrained and who has broken his vows should live on the charity of the land.[2]

3.

If thou art filled with the dread of suffering, if there is naught agreeable for thee in suffering, do then no evil thing openly, or even in secret.

4.

If thou hast done evil deeds, or if thou wouldst do them, thou mayest arise and run where'er thou wilt, but thou canst not free thyself of thy suffering.

---

[1] I have translated in accordance with the Commentary. The text of the Bst. reads the second line, as does the Pâli, "he who scoffs (*spyo-ba-yi*) at the other world." The Commentary and the text of the Bkh. read *bchom-pa-yi*, "gaining."

[2] See on these verses, which, according to the comment, are from the famous Sermon on Falsehoods spoken to Râhula, the Appendix; and for a different version, Beal, *loc. cit.*, p. 142.

5 (127).

There exists no spot on the earth, or in the sky, or in the sea, neither is there any in the mountain-clefts, where an (evil) deed does not bring trouble (to the doer).

6.

When one has looked at those around him and has seen their wicked deeds,[1] let him not do likewise; walk not in the way of sin.

7.

He who commits crimes,[2] who uses false measures,[3] who hurts men, or who does any other similar deeds, will by walking in this path fall into a precipice.

8.

Whatsoever a man has done, whether it be virtuous or sinful deeds, there are none that are of little importance; they all bear some kind of fruit.[4]

9.

As long as men are united, so long will they be the conquerors; but if they would be victorious by other means, they will find out that they will be conquered.[5]

10.

The fool who sees not this walks on in his wicked way, but he who does evil will find out his (mistake) in the other world.[6]

---

[1] "King Adjatasatru had put to death a man who had stolen a fourth of a Karçapana, and another who was an adulterer."—P.

[2] Lit. "very evil deeds," such as killing, &c.—P.

[3] "Who deceives with his metal weights."—P.

[4] Comp. Manu, iv. 234.

[5] Prasenajit and Adjatasatru were not on friendly terms, so Adjatasatru carried off all Prasenajit's elephants, &c. The Bhixus, on going into the town to beg, heard of this event and told Bhagavat, who spoke to them recommending conquering enmity.—P. I have followed the Commentary in translating this verse more than the literal sense that can be derived from a verbatim translation; text also is very uncertain.

[6] According to P., verses 10-14 were spoken on the same occasion.

11 (136).

The fool sees not that his evil deeds, when they shall have matured, will still be burning. Hereafter his deeds will torment him as if burnt by fire.

12 (66).

The fool of little understanding treats himself as he would an enemy; he does evil deeds which will bear burning[1] fruit.

13 (67).

The deed which harms, and of which the reward is received with tears and a downcast face, that deed is not well done.

14 (68).

The deed which harms not, and of which the reward is received with joy and happiness, that deed is well done.

15 (69).

When a man in the pursuit of his pleasure accomplishes an evil deed, it brings smiles to his face; but when his evil deed has ripened, it brings him sorrow.[2]

16 (71).

Surely an evil deed does not turn on a sudden like milk;[3] it is like fire smouldering in the ashes, which burns the fool.

17.

An evil deed kills not instantly, as does a sword, but it follows the evil-doer (even) into the next world.

---

[1] *Hbras-bu tsar.* In Tibetan *tsa,* "salt," and *tsa,* "hot," are only distinguished by a *razur* or small triangle under the word. which is often omitted. The Páli is *katukapphalam,* "bitter fruit."

[2] I have not been able to translate this literally, "like a smile," "like a cry." *Madhura* in the Páli, translated very freely by Professor Max Müller by "honey," means "agreeable, savoury." *Dyong* is explained by P. as "that which is beautiful" (*ldsum-pa-dang-ldan pa*).

[3] *Hgyur* admits to a certain extent of the double sense given to the Páli "*muccati,*" "to get rid of, to curdle." The Commentary explains *hgyur* by *dsor-hgyur,* "to be transformed." Cf. Manu, iv. 172.

18.

How burning is (an evil deed) when it has arrived at maturity, the evil-doers will find out in the other world.

19 (240).

As[1] iron, when the rust doth take hold of it, is eaten by it, so in like manner is the heedless man brought into the evil way by his own deed.

Chapter on Deeds, the Ninth.

---

[1] This verse was spoken at Djetâvana for the edification of the Sthaviras, and of Akroçaka, Roçaka, and Parivaçaka.

X.

FAITH.

1.

FAITH, modesty, morality, charity, these virtues [1] are lauded by holy men;[2] by them one goes to the world of the gods; this road, I declare, leads to the land of the gods.

2 (177).

The avaricious go not to the world of the gods (devas), for the fool commends not charity: they who are steadfast rejoice greatly in charity, also they enjoy happiness in the other (world).

3.

Faith is the greatest treasure of man in this (world),[3] for he who in this (world) observes this law finds happiness: truth has the sweetest of all flavours, and to live according to knowledge is, I declare, the best of lives.

4.

If the wise man has faith in the doctrine of the Arhats[4] that leads to nirvâna,[5] and if he listens respectfully, he will acquire that knowledge.[6]

---

[1] *Tchos* = dharma, explained by *yon-tan*, "good quality, acquirement."
[2] "By the Buddha and his disciples."—P.
[3] Comp. Beal, Dham., p. 52.
[4] *Dgra-bchom tchos* = the way taught by the Buddha.—P.
[5] That causes to find emancipation.—P.
[6] The knowledge of the (four) truths, of the skandhas, of the dhatus, of the ayatanas, &c.—P.

5.

By earnestness one is saved from the ocean,[1] and by faith from out the river; by earnestness misery is removed; by wisdom one is purified.

6.

The Bhixu whose associate is faith and who is full of wisdom will cut off all his bonds for the sake of attaining nirvâṇa.

7.

The wise man who has real faith, morality, wisdom, and who does keep them present in his mind, casts off all sins; he, I declare, is in the good way.

8.

He who has perfect faith and morality, who casts off all avarice, and is liberal,[2] wheresoever he goes, he will be honoured.

9.

The wise man in this world holds fast to faith and wisdom; these are his greatest treasures; he casts aside all other riches.

10.

He who likes to look on holy men, who delights to hear the Law, who has cast away the stains of avarice, he must be called "faithful."

11.

One must lay up provisions of faith; for it is not possible to deprive one of his lot of merit, and one need have no fear of the robbing of thieves. Happy are the Çramaṇas who have acquired it, and happy is the wise man when he meets with (such) a Çramaṇa.[3]

---

[1] The ocean of the three evil ways (regions of desire), and the river of sin (kleça).—P.

[2] *Gtong ldan*, which the Commentary explains as if it were *gtong-sems-ldan*, "he who gives what he possesses."

[3] Comp. vi. 5.

12 (249).

Men give according to their inclination or according to their faith. He whose mind is made unhappy by what another eats and drinks finds no composure[1] by day or night.

13 (250).

He who has put an end to this (feeling), as he would cut off the top of a tala-tree,[2] finds composure by day and by night.

14.

One must not associate with him who is without faith, for he is like a dried-up well, which, if it be dug out, only gives muddy, dirty water.

15.

Let the wise associate with the faithful, who are like a great and limpid river,[3] like a cool and untroubled lake.

16.

The Muni is affected[4] by those who have kindly feelings, or by those who have them not; have then nothing to do with the unfaithful, and associate with the faithful.

Chapter on Faith, the Tenth.

---

[1] *Samadhi,* "he will be troubled by envy."—P. Comp. Pâli "*samâdhim abhigacchati.*"

[2] When the top of the tala-tree has been cut off, it does not grow again.—P.

[3] Where crows gather together (?).—P.

[4] *De-yi thub sku-mi-ngas-pas.* The last four words seem to mean "made ill, infected by." *Tchags sam ma-tchags* the Commentary explains by "those who have faith, or those who have not faith." I have translated it by "kindly feelings." We are told that the origin of this verse was the following event:—Cariputra and Maudgalyayana had left their forest retreat, and had gone into a Brahman village to beg. Some Tirthikas scoffed at them, and in the wickedness of their hearts they filled the alms-bowls with dust, but other Brahmans, who were kindly disposed, gave proper offerings. To the first is reserved the misery of hell, to the second the joy of heaven. *Tchags* refers to the latter, and *ma-tchags* to the former.

XI.

THE ÇRAMANA.[1]

1 (383).

CAST off desires, O Brâhmana, stop the stream (of birth) by thy earnestness; he who is not able to cast away all desires cannot find the one[2] (perfect state).

2 (313).

The irresolute and careless Parivrâdjakas only heap up sins again and again;[3] he who is diligent and earnest knows how to do that which ought to be done.

3 (312).

An irresolute act, badly performed penance, an unrighteous life, bring no great profit.[4]

4 (311).

If an arrow is badly grasped, it cuts the hand; the Çramana who performs his duties badly[5] is on the way to hell.

5.

If an arrow is properly grasped, it does not cut the

---

[1] One who does meditate (*dgong-pa rigs*), not simply a Brâhmana or a Muni.—P.

[2] The nirvâna of the complete destruction of all the skandhas.—P.

[3] *Kun-tu-rgyu-ba-dsan-pa*, compare the Pâli, *sathilo hi paribbâjo bhiyyo âkirate rajam*. The Tibetan has used *ñon-mongs* for *rajam*, whereas it generally translates this term by *rdul*, "dust."

[4] *Tsangs-spyod yongs-su ma-dag-pa*, an exact copy of the Pâli expression *sankassaram brahmacariyam*.

[5] Who observes not the çila precepts.—P.

hand; in like manner, the Çramana who exactly performs his duties is on the way to nirvâṇa.

6.

The ignorant Çramana, who finds it hard to cross (the stream), hard to be patient, who is filled with the many sorrows that his faint-heartedness brings him:

7.

The Çramana whose life is like this, is subject to the ever-recurring grief, of which he cannot free himself, of one who is filled with indecision.

8.

He who is a bad priest, who delights in sin, and who, as a layman, is given to sinful deeds, addicted to everything that is bad, he lays up for himself the wretchedness of regeneration.

9.

Many of those who wear the patched saffron-coloured gown are unrestrained and delight in wickedness; these bad men go to perdition.[1]

10 (162).

He who, breaking all his vows, (is held) as is a sâla-tree by a creeper,[2] brings himself to that state to which his enemy would like to bring him.

11 (260).

Though one's hair may be grey, one is not for that reason admitted among the elders; he has reached old age,[3] but he is called "Old-in-vain."

---

[1] Having departed this life, they fall into the evil way.—P. That is to say, they are born in an inferior condition, as an animal, a demon, &c., or in hell.

[2] He who is entwined in the folds of sin as is the sâla-tree by the wide-spreading creeper.—P.

[3] *Lang-tso gtugs-pa ste.* Although all the lexicons translate *lang-tso* by "youth," it is evidently used here for the Pâli *vayo* (*paripakko vayo*

12 (261).

He who is virtuous, who has cast off sin, who is a Bramachârin, and free of all (impurities), he is called "an elder."

13 (264).

He whose conduct is bad[1] and who speaks lies, though his head be shaven, is not a Çramana. They who live in ignorance and lust, how can they be Çramanas?

14 (265).

He whose conduct is bad and who speaks lies, though his head be shaven, is not a Çramana; he who has "quieted" sin, him the wise know to be a Çramana.[2]

15.

He whose conduct is bad and who speaks lies, though his head be shaven, is not a Çramana; but he who, having distinguished all sins, great and small, does keep away from them and does " quiet " sin, he is called " a Çramana."

16.

He who has "cast off sin" is a Brâhmana; he who does "quiet" sin is a Çramana; he who has cast off all his impurities is for that reason called a priest.[3]

Chapter on " The Çramana," the Eleventh.

---

tassa), which is also used for "youth, any period of life." See Childers, s.v., p. 561. So also *ryam-blun*, "old and foolish," is, according to the Commentary, *rgas-pa don-med-par gyur pa*, "having become old for no purpose." Comp. *moghajinno* in Pâli, in which *mogha* signifies "vain, useless, foolish." See Appendix; comp. Book of Wisdom, iv. 8, 9, and Manu, ii. 156.

[1] Verses 13–15 were spoken in answer to a question of the Brahman Rohitaka. " Bad conduct " means he who does not keep the precepts of the Pratimoxa.—P.

[2] See Max Müller's note on this verse, Dhammapada, p. 65.

[3] In Nâgârjuna's Commentary on the *Dharmadhâtugarbha* (Bstan-hgyur, vol. lxxii. fol. 245) we find these definitions repeated. "He is a Çramana because he quiets sin and pain (kleça). He has cast off all sin, and is therefore a Brâhmana. He has removed his imperfections, and is thus a priest (*rab-tu-byung*)," &c.

XII.

THE WAY.

1.

WHEN one's wisdom has brought him to see the four holy truths, the knowledge of this way will destroy all love of existence.

2.

As the dust [1] is raised by the wind and is laid by the falling rain, in like manner he who has the eye of wisdom, his whole mind is at rest.

3.

That knowledge which enables one to put an end to birth and death, and by which one is freed of the world, that is the best [2] (kind of knowledge).

4 (273).

Among [3] truths the four truths (are the best); the eight-fold way is the best of ways; the best of bipeds is he who sees; the greatest of virtues (dharma), passionlessness.

5 (277).

"All created things [4] are impermanent;" when one has

---

[1] *Rdul,* "dust and passion." The latter part of this verse may be rendered "all indecision is overcome."

[2] The holy eightfold way.—P.

[3] Bhagavat was residing at Rájagriha in the grove of Âmrapâli. A young physician came and saluted Bhagavat and spoke this verse:—
"The best of fruits is the âmalaka (*skyu-ru*);
The best of herbs, the tsitraka (*Ricinus communis*);
The best of fluids, sweets;
The best of salts, rock salt (*rgyam tsa*)."
Bhagavat answered, &c.—P.

[4] In the Páli, *sabbe sankhárá aniccá.* The Tibetan version uses *hdu-byed* throughout for *sankhára;* frequently it must be rendered by "body."

seen this through knowledge, he is no longer afflicted by pain : this is the way to perfect purity.

6 (278).

"All created things are grief;" when one has seen this through knowledge, he is no more afflicted by pain : this is the way to perfect purity.

7 (279).

"All created things are empty (çunyata);" when one has seen this through knowledge, he is no more afflicted by pain : this is the way to perfect purity.

8.

"All created things are unreal;"[1] when one has seen this through knowledge, he is no more afflicted by pain: this is the way to perfect purity.

9 (276).

I have taught you that this way cuts off the pain of existence. The Tathâgata is a teacher; you yourselves must strive after (nirvâna).

10.

I have taught you that this way removes the pain of passion. The Tathâgata is a teacher; you yourselves must strive after (nirvâna).

11 (274).

There is no other road but this one that leads to perfect enlightenment; by concentrating your mind on it you will cast off the bonds of Mâra.[2]

---

[1] *Bag-med-par* = anâtma. Seeing that all corruptions participate of the condition of unreality, and as all conditions (*tchos*) are dependent, old age and death, like desires, are made and occupy one. This is the knowledge that that which is misery does not constitute the self (atma); it is the truth of (the existence of) misery.—P.

[2] Comp. vi. 20.

12.

This way is straight: it leads one to the other world; it is the one road to the ocean of purity. Çakyamuni, well composed and wise, expounds this again and again to the multitude.[1]

13.

Having[2] discovered the ending of birth and death, through kindness and compassion I will teach the way, the only road. After having crossed the stream (of sin), I will teach others to cross as I have crossed.

14.

The way to reach complete cessation (from existence),[3] control, purity; the way to put an end to the recurrence of birth and death; the means of distinguishing all the dhâtus:[4] that is what he who has the eye (of wisdom) teaches by this way.

15.

As the waters of the Ganges flow swiftly on and empty into the ocean, so likewise he who walks in the even way of perfect knowledge shall arrive at the cessation of death.[5]

16.

He who, through compassion towards all creatures, does turn the wheel of the law, heretofore unheard, the Pro-

---

[1] Çakyamuni explained this (way) while seated on the diamond throne (vadjrâsana, *i.e.*, under the Bodhi tree).—P. This verse appears to be the work of Dharmatrâta, and not a gâthâ attributed to Gotama.

[2] This verse, the Commentary says, was spoken while Bhagavat was at Uruvilva, on the bank of the Narandjana river, a short time after he had obtained the all-penetrating and perfect enlightenment. Comp. Mahâvagga, i. 1.

[3] A parivrâdjaka called Rdje-ngar sbom po (thick ankle?) had asked Bhagavat what his system (marga) taught.—P.

[4] *Khams-rnams du-ma so-sor rtogs*, "to perfectly distinguish thought (sankalpa) and nature (svabhâva), conditions (*gnas*) and not conditions, the seven manners of existence," &c.—P.

[5] He shall find the cessation of the fear of death, &c.—P.

tector, the teacher of gods and men, he who has arrived at the end of corporeal existence, him do (I) worship.[1]

17.

By obtaining the perception of the three happinesses,[2] and by casting off the three unhappy things,[3] one will by these perceptions, and by attending to them, arrive at peace : (it is) as the dust (râga) laid by the rain, when the mind and manner are at peace, one then enjoys the felicity of the unsurpassable bodhi.[4]

18.

His mind attached to the three kinds of samâdhi,[5] he meditates in solitude on the (four) immeasurables ;[6] thus does the reflective and wise man undo the knots,[7] and tear (himself away) from the three regions[8] (of desire) by means of the three.[9]

19.

He who has wisdom for a weapon, diligence as his might, who is reflective,[10] well composed, and who delights in meditation (samâdhi), having comprehended the origin and destruction of worldly (existence), will obtain perfect emancipation : he who has comprehended the end-

---

[1] The âgamas say that a deva said, "Sthavira Kaundinya, induce Bhagavat to turn the wheel of the Law."—P. This verse was consequently spoken by Kaundinya and not by Bhagavat. Perhaps, instead of translating *lung* by *âgama*, it ought to be taken as an abbreviation of *lung-bstan* or *vyâkarana*.

[2] *Dge-ba gsum* = the real delivery (from transmigration), &c.—P.

[3] *Dge-ba ma-yin gsum*, i.e., desire, evil mind (*gnod-sems*), hurtfulness (*rnam-par htse-ba*).—P.

[4] In possession of the yoga and the dhyâna he will find the felicity of the extinction of desire (trichnâ), or the felicity of having assumed calmness of mind.—P. *Cf.* xii. 2.

[5] The void, the uncharacteristic, the without longing (*smon-pa med-pa*).—P.

[6] Kindness, mercy, exertion, indifference. Jäschke, s.v. "Tsad," and Commentary, fol. 230b.

[7] *Mdud*, covetousness, &c., sin in general. The root of transmigration, according to the âgamas.—P.

[8] The three regions of living beings or the three evil ways (ngan-song).—P.

[9] Morality, meditation (samâdhi), and wisdom (pradjnâ), these are the three constituent parts of the holy way.—P.

[10] *Dran-ldan*, smriti, the seventh branch of the eightfold way.

ing of worldly (existence), he, I declare, is called "one who has put an end to worldly (existence) and has arrived at the other (shore)."

20.

He whose mind is concentrated on the holy eightfold way, the straight way, has found the immortal (lit. amrita); by following it he finds the much-longed-for happiness, and by finding what is so praiseworthy he increases (his) fame.[1]

Chapter on " The Way," the Twelfth.

---

[1] The last line is *sñan-pa thob-ching grags-pa hphel-bar-hgyur.* I think that my translation agrees with the explanations of the Commentary, but the essential words of the phrase are unfortunately effaced in my copy.

BOOK II.

Book II.

XIII.

HONOURS (SATKÂRA).

1.

As the she-mule (dies) on account of her offspring, as the reed and the plantain decay on bearing fruit, so likewise is the foolish man [1] destroyed by honours.[2]

2 (72).

No matter how long the fool sacrifices, he will not cease from being infatuated; the fool's bright lot [3] goes on decreasing until it brings to sorrow even the crown of his head.[4]

3 (73).

The fool [5] wishes for riches, for the subjection of the Bhixus (to his orders), for lordship [6] in the abode (of the clergy), to receive the homages of other people.

---

[1] *Pho-shal,* "a contemptible, foolish man."—P. This word is not in the dictionaries.

[2] Devadatta and his five hundred followers were receiving from the king of Mâgadha many presents and marks of honour. Bhagavat spoke verses 1 and 2 to illustrate how injurious these riches, &c., were.—P. "The female mule on bringing forth dies, she and her offspring. When therefore she is on the point of bringing forth, a person who is aware of the fact pierces her side with a knife (?) and takes the embryo, otherwise it would die also."—P. "When the plantain produces its fruit, called *mo-rtsa,* the plantain decays and dries up."—P. The same explanation applies to the reed or bamboo. *Cf.* Hitopadesa, ii. çl. 148.

[3] *Dkar-poi-tcha* is the exact translation of the Pâli *sukkamso.*

[4] *Spyi-bo.* Comp. the Pâli *muddhâ,* "the head, top, summit."

[5] Lit. the wicked *ngan,* but the Commentary tells us that it is to be understood as synonymous with *pho-shal* in the preceding verse.

[6] *Ser-sna byed-pa,* "to be avaricious," according to the dictionaries; but as it is here used for the Pâli *issariyam,* we must suppose it can mean "being lord or ruler," or the Tibetan translator may have been misled by *îrchya* (Pâli *issâ*), "envy."

4 (74).

"Let both priests and laymen, whosoever they may be, imagine that it is I (who have done it); in whatever is to be done or not done, let them be subject to me;" such is the mind of the fool, and his desires greatly increase.[1]

5 (75).

One is the way to wealth, another is the road to nirvâṇa; if the Bhixu, the disciple of the Buddha, has learnt this, he finds no pleasure in honours, but seeks after perfect seclusion[2] (from the world).

6.

Retain no fondness for anything; deceive no man;[3] give up any occupation;[4] in (following) the law one must not be engaged in commerce.

7.

Look after what is to your own profit and envy not what is to that[5] of another, for the Bhixu who does envy another cannot find tranquillity (samâdhi).

8.

If a Çramana aspires to lead a happy life, let him put on the gown (sanghâti) of the priesthood and receive alms of food and drink.

9.

If a Çramana aspires to lead a happy life, let him keep

---

[1] His covetousness and pride, which are the root of transmigration, do increase.—P.

[2] Lit. "he increases gradually (his) seclusion;" in Pâli, *virekam anubrâhaye*.

[3] "By informing men of your own qualities, by boasting your own qualities."—P. This refers, P. goes on to say, to observing the çila precepts. The Bhixu who is virtuous and who keeps the çila precepts would not tell a lie for a hundred thousand karshapaṇas, whereas he who thinks of but profit and honours would tell a lie for a single karshapaṇa.

[4] Such as that of king, &c.—P.

[5] The good works that another may have.—P.

to a dwelling-place (of the priesthood), as the reptile does to the rat's hole.¹

10.

If a Çramana aspires to lead a happy life, let him be contented with the meanest things,² and think only of the greatest of laws.³

11.

Though one does not know much, if one keeps well the moral precepts, leading (such) a life according to his knowledge, men say of him in praise, "he is not heedless."⁴

12.

If one possesses the three spotless sciences that overcome the lord of death,⁵ the fool thinks he knows nothing, and that he can blame him.

13.

He who is under the rule of misery and sin, if he has but food, drink, and wealth, him the fool will praise.

14.

He whose head is shaven, and who wears the saffron-coloured gown, but who seeks only for food, drink, clothes, and bedding,⁶ is his greatest enemy.

15.

When, therefore, one knows the sinfulness and danger of honours, with but few desires, and having cast away all agitation of the mind, the reflective Bhixu wanders here and there.

---

¹ As a reptile like the ichneumon (*neu-le*, Sansk. *nevala*), pushed by fear, runs into a rat's hole to protect itself against what it apprehends, in like manner does he who is pursued by misery and desires seek a dwelling-place of the holy disciples, such as a vihâra, &c.—P.

² Such as food, clothing, &c.—P.

³ The law by which one obtains freedom.—P.

⁴ Verses 11–13 are to teach that "you are not to boast of your virtues nor to conceal your sins, for thus you increase your righteousness."—P.

⁵ Perfect understanding, wisdom, (djâna) of the world, and wisdom of delivery from the world.—P.

⁶ The three requisites of the body.—P.

16.

The mind cannot become dispassionate with but a scrap of food, for one must eat to retain this life; he, consequently, who knows that this body only exists through eating, goes to collect alms.

17.

This is what the wise reverence and honour: the removal of every atom of the grief of misery, which is a difficult task, and men honour him who is patient and painstaking; learn, therefore, how to recognise the swamp[1] (and to keep away from it).

Chapter on Honours, the Thirteenth.

---

[1] He who falls in the swamp does sink; so it is with him who seeks wealth and honours; he falls into sin or misery.— P.

XIV.

HATRED.

1.

HATRED towards those who do no evil and who do not hate, this is the sign (lit. garment) of the sinner in this world and in the other.

2.

After having brought misery on himself, he would afterwards bring trouble to others, like unto the hunting hawk, (?)[1] who, captive himself, does injury to others.[2]

3.

He who smites will be smitten; he who shows rancour will find rancour; so likewise from reviling comes reviling, and to him who is angered comes anger.[3]

4.

Those foolish çramanas who know not the holy law, though this life be brief, in the foolishness of their hearts they give themselves to wrangling.

---

[1] *Khra-yis gzan-mai bya*, a bird the extremities of whose wings have been clipped. When a bird like a çarika, &c., draws nigh, it pounces on it and puts it to death.—P.

[2] Verses 1 and 2 were spoken on account of the cries of Devadatta, suffering in hell's fire, or, as others say, on account of the massacre of the Çâkyas by Virûdhaka.—P. Virûdhaka, son of Prasenajit (according to Wassilieff, Târanâtha, p. 287. Prasenajit's son was called Nanda), dethroned his father, and nearly exterminated the Çâkyas; he died in a conflagration. See Dulva, x. 140-160.

[3] Comp. xxvi. 3, and Dham. 133.

5.

"This is the best (man)," they think, being thus at variance with the unanimous opinion: "Why does the clergy choose this man? he is without strength and without mind."

6.

If a bone is broken, (they advise) killing, carrying off horses, cattle, and riches, subduing kingdoms, and then afterwards to become friends again.[1]

7–8.

But the wise man, who knows what is (right), says: "Why do you not learn this law, which teaches the real way to live?" (lit. field of activity). You who have not the conduct of sages, watch carefully over the words of your mouth;[2] guard those of your neighbours who do not know (the danger they may run); they who know (this law), speak soft-toned pleasing words."

9 (3).

"He abused me, he reviled me, he beat me, he subdued me;" he who keeps this in his mind, and who feels resentment, will find no peace.

10 (4).

"He abused me, he reviled me, he beat me, he subdued me;" he who keeps not this in his mind, and is not resentful, will find peace.

---

[1] This verse, as well as several of the others, were spoken in illustration of the conduct of King Brahmadatta of Kaçi and Dirgila (sic) of Koçala, who were enemies. It is to show the fickleness of the foolish man's doings, who, for a mere nothing, commits much evil, and who ends by doing that which ought to have been his first act. This (ver. 6) is the advice given by foolish priests, but the Commentary does not explain it this way; from ver. 7, however, I think there can be no doubt about it.

[2] *Kha-bya-yis ni rtsol-byed-pa.* I fear I have not perfectly understood the remark of the commentator on the first two words. He says, "*Dses bya-ba ni yti-mug-gi dbang-yis rjes-su mthun-pai mtchog ñams-ja ni kha-bya dses-brdjod-de, kha-ni khai-syoo.*"

HATRED.

11 (5).

He who shows hatred to those who hate will never be at peace;[1] he who is patient with those who hate will find peace; this is the spirit of religion.[2]

12.

He who bears ill-will to those who bear ill-will can never become pure; but he who feels no ill-will, pacifies them who hate: as hatred brings misery to mankind, the sage knows no hatred.

13 (328).

If a man find a wise companion,[3] who is both steadfast and pure, let him, having overcome all corruption, associate with him, thoughtful and glad.[4]

14 (329).

If a man find not a wise companion, who is both steadfast and pure, like a king abandoning his broad kingdom,[5] let him live alone and commit no sin.

15 (61).

If a man find not a good friend who leads a life like unto his own, let him resolutely keep a solitary life, and not associate with a fool.[6]

---

[1] Spoken to a female demon (râkchasi).—P.

[2] *Tchos-kyi rang-bdsin*, lit. "the nature of the dharma;" but the Commentary tells us that this idea of patience has belonged to the teaching of all the Buddhas.

[3] A physician of Râjagriha having two sons, had allowed one to enter the sixfold congregation (Buddhist), the other the sect of Kapbina (Kapila?); the latter had fallen among evil companions, the former had found virtuous friends. Bhagavat spoke vers. 13 and 14 in connection with this event.—P.

[4] Comp. Sutta Nipâta, 44 (Khaggavisâna Sutta, 11).

[5] As a king who has faith in the law gives up his kingdom which reaches to the four oceans.—P. Fausböll's translation from the Pâli has "his conquered kingdom." Comp. Sutta Nipâta, 45.

[6] Such as Devadatta, Adjatasatru, Virûdhaka, &c., according to the Commentary.

16 (330).

It is better to live a lonely life than to have companionship with the fool; casting off all taxation of mind, one lives alone, like the elephant of the Mâtanga forest.[1]

Chapter on Hatred, the Fourteenth.

---

[1] *Ma-tang dgon-pai glang po ltar.* The Commentary explains this by saying: "Formerly a richi called Mâtanga lived in this forest." Comp. the Pâli, *mâtangarañño va nâgo.* "Taxation of mind" (*sems-khral*) is also exactly copied on the Pâli *apposukko.*

XV.

REFLECTION (SMRITI).

1.

It is the teaching of the Buddha, that whoever (commences by) reflecting on the operation of breathing, and who goes on through the different stages[1] (of meditation), his mind well composed, will reach perfection, as the sun and moon, when free from clouds, illuminate the whole world.

2.

He who, standing, sitting, and sleeping, keeps both body and mind under control, such a thoughtful and well-controlled Bhixu will find the above-mentioned and other blessings;[2] and if he has obtained the above-mentioned and the other blessings, he will not go to where is the lord of death.

3.

He who continually reflects on what appertains[3] to the body, and has well under control the six senses (âyatanas), and who is always well composed, knows the extinction of sorrow.

---

[1] The six stages (*rnam-pa drug*) are the different steps by which one becomes free from all the imperfections of mankind. See, on this mode of meditation, Giri Ananda Sûtra, Mdo, xxx. ff. 447, 448.

[2] *Snya phyii khyad-par-rnams ni thob-par-hgyur.* The Commentary says *snya* refers to the perfection mentioned in the first verse, and *phyi* to "the discovery of the knowledge of birth and destruction, of impermanency," &c. The "other blessings," or literally "the following," are mentioned in ver. 3.

[3] The text of the Bkah-hgyur has *rtogs* in this and the next verse, but it is evidently a mistake for *gtogs*.

4.

He who continually reflects on what appertains to the body in all its different shapes, on being without self, without attachment for the "mine," will not care for self; he will have no attachment for the "mine:" in this manner will the Bhixu swiftly cross over from the regions of desire.

5.

He who is thoughtful, wise, well composed, happy,[1] and pure, and who attends carefully at all times[2] to this law, will, I declare, cross over from birth and old age.

6.

Thus learning to be always on his guard, the wise, thoughtful, and diligent Bhixu, after having cast off all bonds, finds by this means the destruction of sorrow (nirvâṇa).

7.

They who are awake can watch better than they who sleep, I tell you; it is better to watch than to sleep, for he who watches has no fear.[3]

8.

He who is watchful and diligent is safe day and night, and he will find the end of pain (kleçâ) in the longed-for cessation of death (nirvâṇa).

9.

They who[4] day and night are reflecting on the Buddha,

---

[1] "Happy," for he who is perfectly virtuous, knowing no repentance, is always happy.—P.

[2] *Dus dus su.* This word is interpreted in the dictionaries by "frequently, now and then;" but these terms cannot, I think, be used in the present case. The Commentary says, "*Dus-dus-su dses bya-ba ni mthar-gyis mngon-par rtogs-par hbyung-ba phyir-ro.*"

[3] *Cf.* v. 16.

[4] According to one account, verses 9, 10, 11, were spoken of a man of Virâta, who having heard of the Buddha, had taken refuge in the three precious ones. According to another authority, they were spoken of a dêvaputra who had been born at Râjagriha as a pig.—P.

and who go to the Buddha for a refuge, these men have the profits of mankind.[1]

10.

They who day and night are reflecting on the law (dharma), and who go to the law for a refuge, these men have the profits of mankind.

11.

They who day and night are reflecting on the church (sangha), and who go to the church for a refuge, these men have the profits of mankind.

12 (296).

The disciple of Gautama is always well awake, day and night reflecting on the Buddha.

13 (297).

The disciple of Gautama is always well awake, day and night reflecting on the law.

14 (298).

The disciple of Gautama is always well awake, day and night reflecting on the church.

15.

The disciple of Gautama is always well awake, day and night reflecting on the laws of morality (çila).

16.

The disciple of Gautama is always well awake, day and night reflecting on renunciation.[2]

17.

The disciple of Gautama is always well awake, day and night reflecting on the way.[3]

---

[1] See note to Vasubhandhu's first gâtha, in the Appendix.
[2] *Gtong-ba* appears to be the accomplishment of the paramitas.
[3] Seeking to free himself of the region of desire and of passions.—P.

18 (299).

The disciple of Gautama is always well awake, day and night reflecting on what appertains to the body.

19.

The disciple of Gautama is always well awake, day and night keeping in mind the four kinds of meditation (samâdhi).[1]

20.

The disciple of Gautama is always well awake, day and night delighting in the cessation of death.

21 (300).

The disciple of Gautama is always well awake, day and night delighting in kindness of heart.

22 (301).

The disciple of Gautama is always well awake, day and night delighting in meditation.

23.

The disciple of Gautama is always well awake, day and night delighting in the unconditioned.[2]

24.

The disciple of Gautama is always well awake, day and night delighting in the uncharacteristic.[3]

25.

The disciple of Gautama is always well awake, day and night delighting in solitude.

---

[1] Divided into two classes—(1.) dhyâna; (2.) indifference (*shoms-par hdjug-pa*).—P. *Cf.* xii. 18. Perhaps "basis (*gdsi*) of meditation" is the correct reading.

[2] *Stong-pa ñid*, *sunyata*, lit. void, emptiness.

[3] *Mtsan-ma-med*. See Wassilieff, Buddh., pp. 293, 298 (French trans.)

26.

The disciple of Gautama is always well awake, day and night delighting in what leads to salvation.[1]

27.

The disciple of Gautama is always well awake, day and night delighting in nothing (worldly ?).

28.

The disciple of Gautama is always well awake, day and night rejoicing in nirvâṇa.[2]

Chapter on Reflection, the Fifteenth.

---

[1] *Nges-par-hbyung-pa, niryânika.* See Childers, s.v. "Niyyâniko."

[2] The nirvâṇa of the destruction of every particle of the skandhas is what he strives and longs for, which, when he has reached, he will have all the felicities of peace.—P.

XVI.

MISCELLANEOUS.

1.

When you feel inclined to do a thing, commence by examining it: "If I had only done thus at first, one wishes when it is too late.

2.

"I would have seen the real nature of desire, and that it becomes a fetter;" let one watch what he does as long as he is striving after perfection.

3 (238).

By application and diligence one will make oneself an island. Remove thine impurities as does the smith those of the silver: thine impurities removed and free from sin, thou shalt find no more birth and old age.[1]

4 (316, 317).

He who is ashamed of what is not shameful, and not ashamed of what is shameful, who fears what is not fearful, and who fears not what is fearful, that man has wrong views and will be lost.

---

[1] Although this verse reproduces also Dham. 239, I take it to be the equivalent of 238, as ver. 10, chap. ii., is a more exact translation of 239 than this one. See, on the origin of these two verses, the Appendix.

5 (172).

He who formerly was heedless and who afterwards has become careful, like the moon free from clouds, he brightens up the whole world.[1]

6.

He who formerly was heedless and who afterwards has become careful will by reflecting leave behind him the desires of this world.

7 (382).

He who has entered the priesthood when young and who follows the doctrines of the Buddha, like the moon free from clouds, he brightens up the whole world.[2]

8.

He who is a young priest and who follows the doctrine of the Buddha will by reflecting leave behind him the desires of this world.

9 (173).

He who covers up his evil deeds by good deeds brightens up the whole of this world like the moon free from clouds.

10.

He who covers up his evil deeds by good deeds will by reflecting leave behind him the desires of this world.

11.

He who delights not in life, finds no sorrow in death; he knows the reward of earnestness, and is without pain even in the midst of sorrow.[3]

---

[1] Verses 5 and 6 were spoken for the edification of King Prasenajit.

[2] Verses 7 and 8 were spoken because King Prasenajit would not believe in young priests, but only in grey-headed men.—P. Bhagavat caused all the priests to appear as if seventy years old, and afterwards they became young as before. This legend is well known.

[3] Verses 11-13 were spoken by Bhagavat on hearing of the massacre of the Çâkyas, his kinsmen. "Reward of earnestness" (*brtan-pa go-hphang*) means, most likely, nirvâṇa in this and next verse.

12.

He who delights not in life finds no sorrow in death; he knows the reward of earnestness, and is a shining light to the rest of his relatives.

13.

The Bhixu who by meditating on virtue has cast off sin leaves his home for a homeless condition, which is the true field of activity, and then, having learnt what is real joy, he casts off every desire.

14.

One whose heart is always pure, pure by always confessing his sins, in every act observing the way of purity, will reach perfection.[1]

15 (356).

'Tis weeds that do damage a field, 'tis passions that damage mankind; he therefore who gives to them who are without passions will receive a great reward.[2]

16 (357).

'Tis weeds that do damage a field,[3] 'tis hatred that does damage mankind; he therefore who gives to them who are without hatred will receive a great reward.

---

[1] A Brahman called Vardvadja-sundarika (sic) said to Bhagavat, "Çramana Gautama, I bathe in the Sundarika river." Bhagavat asked him, "Brahman, what is the use of bathing in the Sundarika river?" "Why, Çramana Gautama, one praises a monument (?) (stegs-ni bsngags-pa yin-te), and one praises the river Sundarika, which is holy. He who bathes in the Sundarika river is cleansed of all his sins." Then Bhagavat answered, &c.—P. fol. 263, vol. lxxi.

[2] A poor man, who had given Subhuti some flour, found a treasure (as a reward). Bhagavat then spoke these verses (15–18). According to another account, Prasenajit asked Bhagavat to whom one ought to make gifts.—P.

[3] Rtsa, "grass," is here used for "bad weeds." Compare the Pâli tiṇa. "Mankind," in Tibetan skye-dgu, lit. "nine men." Compare with such plural forms the Chinese wen-min, "nations," pe-kuan, "magistrates," &c.

17 (358).

'Tis weeds that do damage a field, 'tis ignorance that does damage mankind; he therefore who gives to them who are without ignorance will receive a great reward.

18.

'Tis weeds that do damage a field, 'tis selfishness that does damage mankind; he therefore who gives to them who are without selfishness will receive a great reward.

19 (359).

'Tis weeds that do damage a field, 'tis lust that does damage mankind; he therefore who gives to them who are without lust will receive a great reward.[1]

20.

'Tis weeds that do damage a field, 'tis desire (trîchnâ) that does damage mankind; he therefore who gives to them who are without desires will receive a great reward.

21.

(These) six[2] are lord and master. If one is given to passion (râga), he has (all) the passions; if one is without passion (râga), he is without (any of) the passions. He who is passionate is called a fool.

22 (150).

When a citadel has been made of bones, plastered over with flesh and blood,[3] passion, hatred, and selfishness dwell together in it.

---

[1] Although we are told that only four verses (15-18) were spoken to illustrate the reward of charity (see note to verse 15), verses 19 and 20 evidently belong to the same sermon.

[2] i.e., passions, hatred, &c.; see the six preceding verses. I have followed the indication of the Commentary in translating this verse. The text uses only the word tchags, but P. says that in the second and fourth cases it is to be understood as "passions, hatred, ignorance, &c."

[3] The Tibetan expression, sha dang khrag-gis dsul-dsul byas, is an exact copy of the Pâli mamsalohitalepanani. Cf. Manu, vi. 76.

23.

They who do not perceive the source from whence comes all their misery are held in bondage; they who have found it out leave the waters (of sin) and cross over to the other side, where they are free from passions.

Chapter on Miscellanies, the Sixteenth.

XVII.

WATER.

1 (91).

THEY who, with all their energy given to reflection, find no pleasure in a home, like a swan[1] who leaves a polluted lake, they leave their homes and cross the stream.

2 (175).

The steadfast depart from the world,[2] having overcome the troops of Mâra; they are like unto swans in the path of the sun, moving in the ether by means of their miraculous power (irddhi).[3]

3 (155).

They who do not live like Brahmatchâris, and who do not acquire wealth in their youth, become like old herons on the banks of a polluted pool with few fish.[4]

---

[1] The text has *ngang*, "goose," but this word is here used as in the Pâli *hamso*, "goose, swan."

[2] *Hjig-rten ngas-byung-nas*. This expression is copied on the Pâli *niyanti lokamha*.

[3] These two verses (1, 2) were spoken on the following occasion:— There was a Brahman called Nyagrodha, whose riches equalled those of Mahâpadma. He owned sixteen villages, thirty slave villages, nine hundred and ninety-nine pair of oxen, sixty koti of treasure, besides eighty gold ear-rings. His son, called Mahâkaçyapa, had not taken a wife, notwithstanding the entreaties of his parents. Finally he said, "If there be a maiden who eclipses this image made of gold of the Jambu river, her will I take." He took as his wife Kapilabhadrâ of Mâgadha, and after a while left her and entered the priesthood, where he obtained the condition of an Arhat.—P. See Dulva, ix. fol. 37–54 where these verses are not, however, occur; and in Schiefner's Tibetan Tales, the story of Mahâkasyapa and Bhadrâ.

[4] "Few fish," *ña ñung;* compare the Pâli *khiṇamacche*.

4 (156).

They who do not live like Brahmatchâris, and who do not acquire wealth in their youth, remembering what they have formerly done, they lie thirsting for the past.

5 (121).

Think not "Evil is of little importance; it will not follow after me;" for as a large vase is filled by the falling of drops of water, so will the fool become full of evil, even if he gathers it little by little.

6 (122).

Think not "Virtue is of little importance; it will not follow after me;" for as a large pot is filled by the falling of drops of water, so will the earnest man become full of virtue, even if he gathers it little by little.[1]

7.

Longing to leave the vast and turbid lake and to cross the waters of the ocean, the wise man is carried across in the vessel that he has prepared.

8.

When he has crossed over,[2] he shall inhabit the promised land of the Enlightened, of the Blessed, of the Brâhmana; therefore let the Bhixus, and they who listen (to my doctrine), washing themselves clean (of sin), make ready a vessel.

9 (82).

The wise and excellent man who listens to the law becomes like a deep, limpid, and pure lake.[3]

---

[1] *Cf.* Hitopadesa, ii. çl. 10.
[2] After having gradually cast off all sin and acquired wisdom. Being free of all human conditions, he is enlightened (*i.e.*, a Buddha).—P.
[3] According to the Commentary this verse ought to come after No. 11.

10.

When there is water everywhere, who is there who would run about seeking the water of a well? What use is there for well water? Destroy then desires from the very roots.[1]

11 (80).

The scourer[2] washes with water, the fletcher straightens (his arrows) with fire, the carpenter hews his logs, the wise man shapes himself.

12.

Passionless as the firmament, firm as the lintel of the door,[3] the wise man delights not in transmigration, which is like a troubled lake.

Chapter on Water, the Seventeenth.

---

[1] This verse is not mentioned in the Commentary.

[2] *Gtso-blag-mkhan* is a man who (uses) *tchu-tchu* (rhubarb?) mixed with water, or, according to others, one who washes and cleans clothes in soda (*bul-tog*) water, &c. — P. Comp. Stan. Julien, Avadânas, i. p. 23.

[3] Comp. Sutta Nipâta, 213, 228.

XVIII.

THE FLOWER.

1 (44).

Who is there that can overcome the world of the gods, of the lord of death (Yama) and of men, who knows how to expose the most delightful law, as one would flowers?[1]

2 (45).

It is the disciple (sekhas) who can overcome the world of the gods, of the lord of death and of men, who knows how to expose the most delightful law, as one would flowers.

3 (283).

Fear is born of the forest (of ignorance); so cut down not (only) the trees of the forest, but all that appertains to the forest (*i.e.*, the roots), and then the Çramana will find nirvâṇa.[2]

---

[1] "Like unto a clever wreath-maker, who, having taken flowers from a garden, has manufactured them into beautiful wreaths and has then given them away, is he who, having gathered a quantity (*gya nom*) of precepts from out the Çastras and formed them into a pleasing collection, does teach them to others.—P. vol. lxxii. fol. 14b. Comp. M. Fausböll's translation: "Quisnam versus legis bene enarratos, peritus (coronarius) flores velut, colliget?" The French translation (Fernand Hû's) appears to me very objectionable: "Qui développera les vers de la Loi, comme on développe adroitement une fleur?"

[2] See on the origin of this verse the Appendix.

4 (284).

If man destroys not everything that appertains to the forest down to the smallest part, his mind will be held in bondage, as the calf that wants milk is to its mother's side.[1]

5 (285).

Cut out the love of self as you would an autumn lotus; cherish the road of peace on account of the nirvâṇa which the Victorious One has explained.[2]

6 (51).

Like a pretty flower, of pleasing colour but without scent, are the agreeably spoken but fruitless words of one who does not act (accordingly).[3]

7 (49).

As the bee, which harms neither the colour nor the scent of the flower, but having sucked it flies away, so let the Muni walk through a village.[4]

8 (50).

Remarking not the sins of others, and what they have done or left undone, one should remark what he himself does right or wrong.

9 (58).

As on piles of filth and in dirty water grows, unaffected by them, the padma, pure, sweet-smelling, and lovely,

---

[1] A disciple called Uttara parasharya, who had given his small possessions to his son, heard of his son's death, the burning of his home, and of great afflictions to many of his relatives. Bhagavat tells him not to be grieved, that disciples ought to be always well composed, &c. *Cf.* iii. 8.

[2] See also Tittha Jâtaka.

[3] Bhagavat walking in a forest saw some *kosnataki* (?) and *donka* plants, which suggested this simile. The *donka* or *don-ga* (according to Jäschke) is "a tropical climbing plant, a sweet-tasted, lenient purgative." According to the Commentary, there ought to be after this verse No. 52 of the Dhammapada; I keep, however, to the text of the Bkah-hgyur, which omits it. Lucian uses the expression $\dot{\alpha}\nu\epsilon\mu\hat{\omega}\nu\alpha\iota\;\lambda\acute{o}\gamma\omega\nu$, "anemony words," to describe senseless verbosity.

[4] See also Pratimoxa Sûtra, 4; Mel. Asiat., viii. pp. 590, 592; and Beal, Catena, p. 159.

10 (59).

So the disciple of the perfect Buddha shines by his wisdom among other men, who are blind and (like) a heap of filth.

11 (53).

As out of a heap of flowers many garlands are made, so when a man has been born he can do many virtuous deeds.

12 (377).

As the vakula[1] plant in summer sheds all its flowers, so let the Bhixu drop passions, hatred, and ignorance.

13 (47).

A man whose mind is troubled, like one gathering flowers, the lord of death carries him off as the flood does a sleeping village.

14 (48).

A man whose mind is troubled, like one gathering flowers, falls into the power of the lord of death without having satisfied his desires.

15.

A man whose mind is troubled, like one gathering flowers, falls into the power of the lord of death without him having acquired wealth (enough to satisfy him).

16.

A man whose mind is troubled, like one gathering flowers, falls into the power of the lord of death without having arrived at the object of his pursuit.

17.

He who has perceived that this body is (empty) as a vase, and who knows that all things (dharma) are as an

---

[1] The *Mimusops Elengi*. The Pâli text has the *vassikâ* plant or "great-flowered jasmine."

illusion, does thus destroy the chief of Mâra's flowers, and will no more be seen by the king of death.

18 (46).

He who has perceived that this world is like froth, and who knows that all things are as an illusion, does thus destroy the chief of Mâra's flowers, and will no more be seen by the king of death.

19.

He who has perceived that this body is like froth, and who knows that all things are as an illusion, does thus destroy the chief of Mâra's flowers, and will no more be seen by the king of death.

20.

(Repetition of verse 18.)

21.

The Bhixu who knows that existence is without reality, like an udumbâra[1] flower, casts off what is and is not of the other shore, as a snake shuffles off his old dried-up skin.[2]

22.

The Bhixu who cuts off every particle of passion, as one does the flower from the water-born (lotus) growing in a tank, casts off what is and is not of the other shore, as a snake shuffles off his old dried-up skin.[3]

23.

The Bhixu who cuts off every particle of hatred, as one does the flower from the water-born (lotus) growing

---

[1] *Ficus glomerata.* "Like one that looks for flowers on fig-trees" Fausböll).

[2] See Uraga Sutta, 5 (Sut. Nip.) Bhagavat was quietly seated near the great lake Ma-dros-pa (Manasa), when perceiving near by a grove of fig-trees (udumbâra trees), he spoke this verse.—P.

[3] See Uraga Sutta, 2.

in a tank, casts off what is and is not of the other shore, as a snake shuffles off his old dried-up skin.

24.

The Bhixu who cuts off every particle of ignorance, as one does the flower of the water-born (lotus) growing in a tank, casts off what is and is not of the other shore,[1] as a snake shuffles off his old dried-up skin.

25.

The Bhixu who cuts off every particle of egotism, as one does the flower of the water-born (lotus) growing in a tank, casts off what is and is not of the other shore, as a snake shuffles off his old dried-up skin.

26.

The Bhixu who cuts of every particle of affection, as one does the flower of the water-born (lotus) growing in a tank, casts off what is and is not of the other shore, as a snake shuffles off his old dried-up skin.

27.

The Bhixu who cuts off every particle of desire, as one does the flower of the water-born (lotus) growing in a tank, casts off what is and is not of the other shore, as a snake shuffles off his old dried-up skin.

Chapter on "The Flower," the Eighteenth.

---

[1] That is to say, the five skandhas. Being on the edge of the world, he strives earnestly to cast off what is opposed to the other world.—P. The text is rather obscure, *pha-rol-min-pai pha-rol-po spong-ste*. According to M. Fausböll's translation, "he leaves this and the farther shore." The Tibetan text might, however, be rendered, "he casts off what is opposed to the other shore." Sir Coomara Swamy translates this phrase by "gives up Orapara."

XIX.

THE HORSE.

1 (144).

If a good horse is struck with a whip, he is frightened and exerts himself with all his strength; so likewise when one is full of faith, morality, and meditation (samâdhi), having never aught to do with the phenomenal world (dharma), having his senses well composed, patient, and glad, thus goaded on he leaves the world completely behind.[1]

2.

If a good horse is struck with a whip, he is frightened and exerts himself with all his strength; so likewise when one is full of faith, morality, and meditation, having never aught to do with the phenomenal world, having knowledge and (observing) the fundamental (rules),[2] thus goaded on[3] he casts away every particle of misery.

3 (143).

They who are well subdued, like well-broken horses, whose senses are so well controlled as to keep down anger, putting thus an end to sorrow, these Munis will soon be rejoicing among the gods.

---

[1] They learn how to acquire the nirvâṇa of the destruction of every particle of the skandhas.—P.

[2] *Rkang-par-ldan*, which the Commentary explains by *tsul-khrims* or morality.

[3] *Skyob-pa de-rnams*, lit. "those protected or those protections." I have forced the meaning so as to bring out my idea of the simile in these two verses.

4.

The pure man has no intercourse with the careless, the vigilant with the slothful, as the good horse who is wise leaves the wild horses and wanders (alone).[1]

5.

He who minds modesty and knowledge as a good horse does the whip, and who is well composed by wisdom, cleanses himself of sin.[2]

6 (321).

The tamed (horse) is made to go to the place of assembly;[3] the king rides the tamed (horse); the best among tamed men is he who patiently endures abuse.

7 (322).

Better than the largest of elephants, than thoroughbred[4] Sindhu horses, than well-broken mules, is he who tames himself.

8 (323).

With one's own well-tamed self one can reach peace, but with these other modes of conveyance it is not possible to reach that state.

9.

Better than the largest of elephants, than thoroughbred Sindhu horses, than well-broken mules, is he who tames himself.

10.

With one's own well-tamed self one can arrive at the

---

[1] Comp. Khaggavisâna Sutta, 19. The simile used in the Pâli version, "let one wander alone like a rhinoceros," is frequently used in the Tibetan Vibhanga. Cf. Bhixuni Vinaya Vibhanga, ff. 90b, 91b, et passim.

[2] Comp. Dham. 143.

[3] Hdun-sar. Compare Pâli dantam nayanti samitim.

[4] The text is Sindui chang-shes rta, which, if we translate according to the lexicons, would imply "all knowing Sindu (sic) horses." I think that we may use the word "thoroughbred" when we take into consideration the Pâli âjânîyâ va sindhavâ. See Childers, s. v. "Âjânâmi" and "Âjânîyo."

end of affliction, but with these other modes of conveyance it is not possible to reach that state.

11.

Better than the largest of elephants, than thoroughbred Sindhu horses, than well-broken mules, is he who tames himself.

12.

With one's own well-tamed self one can cast off humanity, but with these other modes of conveyance it is not possible to reach that state.

13.

Better than the largest of elephants, than thoroughbred Sindhu horses, than well-broken mules, is he who tames himself.

14.

With one's own well-tamed self one will depart, having severed one's bonds, but with these other modes of conveyance it is not possible to reach that state.

15.

He who would be tamed like a good horse must tame himself; with the self well tamed one reaches the end of affliction.

16.

Self is the lord of self; self is the refuge of self: therefore break the self as you would a good horse.[1]

Chapter on " The Horse," the Nineteenth.

---

[1] Spoken for the instruction of an old merchant of Veratya (Virâta?), who, being an object of scorn to his children, &c., asked (Bhagavat) who was the master.—P.

XX.

ANGER.

1 (221).

WHEN one has cast off anger, cast off selfishness, leaving behind every description of bondage, without any fondness for name and form, free from everything,[1] he cannot fall into the way of passions.

2.

Casting away rising anger, casting away the passions as soon as they show themselves, the steadfast man casting away all ignorance, will find happiness in the perception of the truth.[2]

3.

If one has cast away anger, his sleep is peaceful; if one has cast away anger, he knows no sorrow. Bhixus, destroy anger, which is the root of the poison; the elect declare that they who have overcome it, are without sorrow.

4.

"There is nothing better than to master one's anger." This is a great saying,[3] for pain comes after anger, as it does when one has been burnt with fire.

---

[1] Having cast off all subjection to desires and ignorance.—P.
[2] The Four Truths.—P.
[3] *Dscs rab smra-ba.* This seems to have been taken from Dhammapada, 227: "*porânam etam atulam.*" These words are not found in the Tibetan version of 227. See chap. xxix. ver. 49.

5.

He who is not chaste, without modesty, who gives way to anger, who is without restraint, he who is thus subdued by passion, who is there that cares for him?[1]

6.

He who has but the strength of the ignorant has a strength which is not one. It is not likely that the fool who knows nothing of the law can attain perfection.[2]

7.

He who having strength is patient with those who are weak, him I call the most patient of men, submitting always to the opinions of the weak.

8.

He who, though he is lord over others,[3] is patient with those who are weak, him I call the most patient of men, submitting always to the opinions of the weak.

9.

He who, having been chided, is patient though he be strong, him I call the most patient of men, submitting always to the opinions of the weak.

10.

He who, knowing that his enemy is angered, remains peaceful himself, preserves himself and others from great dangers.

---

[1] He is like a poisonous black snake, which nobody will take, love, or admit in their dwelling.—P.

[2] A Brahman of Çravasti called Giriya-gro (?) carried (on his back) a sâla-tree and laid it down before King Prasenajit. Bhagavat coming there after a while (the king said), "Venerable one, I have a very strong man here." Then Bhagavat answered, &c.—P. The fool cannot attain the happiness of those who are virtuous and who walk in the way.—P.

[3] The Commentary reads, "a mighty lord."

11.

He who, knowing that his enemy is angered, remains peaceful himself, does that which is beneficial both to himself and to the other.

12.

He who acts thus for the benefit of himself and others, they who know not the law, lightly think "He is a fool!"

13.

The words of the superior man are patient through fear (of the consequences); the patience that endures abuse and provocations, which endures humiliating words, that patience is the best, the sage says.

14.

The fool who is angered and who thinks to triumph by using abusive language, is always vanquished by him whose words are patient.

15 (224).

Speak the truth; yield not to anger; give to him who begs, even though it be but a little: by living up to these three (rules of conduct) thou wilt go to the abode of the gods.[1]

16.

He who is overcome by anger sees not what is good for himself; if you would free yourself of transmigration, speak not angry words.

17.

He who, having been angered, gives way to anger again, is sinful; but he who, having been angered, gives way to it no more, has won a mighty victory.

---

[1] Verses 15, 16, and 17 were spoken to an old priest who was avaricious and cheaty, and who had taken an old worn-out cloak and had dyed it and fixed it so as to look as if it had just been made. Rebuked by Maudgalyayana, he seeks Bhagavat, who speaks the words of the text. See Baka Jâtaka.

ANGER.

18 (223).

Overcome anger by not being angered; overcome evil by good; overcome avarice by liberality; overcome falsehoods by truth.[1]

19.

He who is controlled and who leads a righteous life, by what could he be angered? The wise, who have perfect wisdom and who are emancipated, are without anger.[2]

20.

The elect associate always with him who is without anger, without wickedness; they who are wicked and given to anger (live alone), weighed down as if by a mountain.[3]

21 (222).

He who holds in rising anger, as he would guide a chariot on the road, him I call an accomplished driver; the vulgar crowd only hold the reins.[4]

Chapter on Anger, the Twentieth.

---

[1] This verse was addressed to a Brahman called Asurayana, or, according to other accounts, to the Upâsikâ Udari, wife of Udara.—P.

[2] According to the Commentary, this verse was spoken to the son of a Brahman who had come to abuse the Blind one. The story is similar to the one given in the Sutra in 42 sections, vii. See Appendix.

[3] The text is *ri-bo bdsin-du sgur-bar-byed*, which is difficult to explain satisfactorily.

[4] *Dsays hdcbs;* compare the Pâli *rasmiggâho.*

XXI.

THE TATHÂGATA.

1.

IN this world I know all, I have conquered all, I am free from all conditions (dharma), I have cast away everything; having put an end to all desires, perfectly emancipated, manifestly wise, by whom can I be taught?

2.

I am the Tathâgata, the highest teacher; I am almighty, omniscient, and have obtained perfect wisdom (bodhi), which I fathomed by myself; incomparable and unequalled, by whom can I be taught?[1]

3.

I am the Arhat of the world;[2] in this world I am unequalled; (alone) among gods and men I have conquered the hosts of Mâra.[3] As there is none other like me, no one can be my master; all alone in the world I have found perfect and unsurpassable wisdom (samyaksambodhi).

4.

I have found the cessation of the âsravas; like unto me are (all) Djinas, who have found this out. I have

---

[1] According to the Commentary, these first two verses are not separated. In fact, nearly all the first part of this chapter is supposed to be one *udâna*, spoken by Gautama shortly after attaining enlightenment. See Appendix. Comp. Mahâvagga, i. 7, 8.

[2] Or, "I have conquered the enemy of the world (Mâra.)"

[3] Comp. Lalita Vistara, chap. xxvi.

overcome all states of sinfulness, therefore am I a Djina.[1]

5.

As I am the conqueror of all that is like (sin), I the all-wise, perfectly enlightened one, who have crossed over from the region of desire, I who have attained nirvâṇa, I am not to be taught by any one in the world.

6.

I am going to Vâraṇasi to sound the Drum of the Law for those who until now have known naught of it, to turn the Wheel of the Law that has been turned by no one in the world.[2]

7.

The mighty Tathâgatas do instruct here[3] by the law; they who have learnt the law, there is no one that can look down on them.

8.

Both gods and men delight in him who is steadfast, who is given to meditation, delighting in the peace of salvation, who has reached the end of corporeal existence,[4] who is Perfectly Enlightened, glorious, and who is in the enjoyment of Wisdom (pradjnâ).

9.

They who have been Buddhas, the future Buddhas,

---

[1] Comp. Mahâvagga, i. 9.
[2] Comp. Mahâvagga, i. 9, and Lalita Vistara, chap. xxvi. p. 379, of M. Foncaux's translation.
[3] "Here" means at Râjagriha.—P. Although the Commentary is here so much effaced that I can hardly read it, I can make out that Upatichya (i.e., Çariputra) had at that time made his profession of faith (dad-dpang-nas ?), and had gone to beg alms, when he was met by a Tirthika who said, "If you carry off everything, what will there be for me?" When he told this to Bhagavat, he said that this was what he must answer on such occasions.
[4] The Devas, perceiving Bhagavat on the Gridhrakuṭa mountain plunged in the calmness of the region of fire, were greatly pleased, and rejoiced, and asked Gautama, how they could attain this perfection.—P.

and the present perfect Buddha, do liberate (mankind) from many sorrows. To reverence the law, for all those who have been, who are, and who shall be, this is the great law of all Perfectly Enlightened ones. He, therefore, who in this world cares about himself, and who wishes to arrive at greatness, let him remember the commandment of the Buddhas and reverence the law.

10.

The man who has no faith in the doctrine of the Buddha is a fool; he will finally come to grief, as did the merchants with the Râkshasîs (female demons).[1]

11.

The man who has faith in the doctrine of the Buddha, and who is wise, will arrive at felicity in the other world, like the merchants (carried off) by "Might of a Cloud."[2]

12.

It is by perfect understanding of happiness and of the value of seclusion, and by living according to both of these, that the unequalled and incomparable Tathâgatas, the perfectly enlightened, dispel darkness, pass over to the other side, and acquire glory (among men).

13.

Their minds all-powerful by having obtained what was to be obtained, perfectly free, having put an end to the âsravas, completely emancipated, mercifully longing to deliver (mankind), without wickedness[3] or âsrava,[4] they show the beings of the universe what is beneficial to them.

---

[1] From the Singhalasûtra.—P. See Hiuen Thsang, Si-yu-ki, xi. pp. 132-140. This Sûtra is not in the Tibetan canon.

[2] *Sprin-gyi shugs-chan*, name of the divine horse from the Trâyastrimcat's heaven, who delivered the merchants from the island of the Râkshasîs. See Hiuen Thsang, loc. cit., p. 133.

[3] *Tha-ba*, such as anger, &c.—P.

[4] Selfishness, ignorance, &c.—P.

14-15.

They who are on the summit of a mountain can see all men; in like manner they who are intelligent and free from sorrow are enabled to ascend above the paradise of the gods; and when they there have seen the subjection of man to birth and death and the sorrows by which he is afflicted, they open the doors of the immortal. Let those who will listen free themselves of all distrustfulness.[1]

Chapter of the Tathâgata, the Twenty-First.

---

[1] These verses were spoken for the edification of Mâhabrahmâ.—P. The last line is explained thus: "They who do not believe in the province (*yul*) of truth, remove them entirely; free yourselves of them; remove all doubt in the (efficiency) of the way that leads to the cessation of death.—P. *Cf.* iv. 4.

XXII.

THE HEARER.

1.

To listen attentively, to live righteously, to give up a home for a state of happiness,[1] to consent to give up all, these are alike praiseworthy in a Çramana.

2.

The fool, who knows not, behaves as if he was immortal; the wise man applies himself day and night to the holy law.

3–4.

If a person enters into a house wrapped in darkness, though he has eyes he cannot see objects that are (in it); so likewise though a man is well born and has intelligence, if he hears not the law of vice and of virtue he cannot have wisdom.

5.

Like a man who, having eyes and who bearing also a lamp, sees all objects, is he who has heard the law of vice and of virtue; he will become perfectly wise.[2]

6.

They who hearken acquire knowledge of the law; they who hearken turn away from sin; they who hearken give up all evil-doers;[3] they who hearken find nirvâna.

---

[1] To enter the priesthood.—P.
[2] Comp. Sutra in 42 sections, sect. xv.
[3] *Don-med spong*, which the Commentary explains by "*sdig-pa-chan gyi skye-bo-mi bsten pao.*"

THE HEARER.

7.

If one has heard much but observes not the moral laws (çîla), he, because he disdains the moral laws, is not the best kind of hearer.

8.

If one has heard little but does carefully observe the moral laws, he, because he honours the moral laws, is the best kind of hearer.[1]

9.

He who listens but little and he who observes not the moral laws, both of these, by reason of their disrespectfulness, lead not the best of lives.

10.

He who has heard and he who carefully observes the moral laws, both of these, by reason of their reverence, lead the best of lives.

11.

They who have heard much and who understand the law, who are wise and well composed, no one can scorn them, for they are like a jewel of gold of Djambudvipa.

12.

He who describes me in his speech, having judged me (only) by outward appearance (lit. form), that man is held by lust and does not know me.[2]

13.

If one has a thorough knowledge of the inner[3] (quali-

---

[1] Comp. verses 7, 8 with iv. 22, 23.
[2] Prasenajit, being very much pleased with the language of one of the disciples, had come to make him a present to where he was with Ananda, but, on drawing nigh, he saw that he had a very repulsive appearance, so he put down his gifts in anger and forthwith went away. Then the Buddha spoke these five verses (12–16).
[3] *Nang*, "that is, the perfections (guna) that are inside, the way to nirvâṇa."—P.

ties of the Buddha), but has not seen the outer [1] (perfections of his person), let him, having perceived the inner fruits, be candid in his language.

14.

If one has seen the outer (perfections of the Buddha),[2] but has not a knowledge of the inner (qualities of his doctrine), let him, having perceived the apparent fruit,[3] be candid in his language.

15.

If one has no knowledge of the inner (qualities), and has not perceived the outer (perfections of my person), a fool in utter darkness, let him be candid in his language.[4]

16.

If one has a thorough knowledge of the inner (qualities), and has seen the outer (perfections), a sage who knows the way to salvation, let him be candid in his language.

17.

Though the ear hears much and the eye sees many things, all they who do hear and see the doctrine, do not believe.

18.

Though a man has inwardly digested the well-spoken words he has heard, and has acquired the essence of meditation, if he acts corruptly his hearing and understanding will avail him nothing.

---

[1] *Phyi-rol*, that is, form (rupa).—P.
[2] The thirty-two signs of the great man, the eighty beauties of his person.—P.
[3] They have seen the perfection of his body.—P.
[4] *Drang-du rung*, if they be believers in false doctrines, let them stay in the right way (the way of truth?). These verses present several difficulties that I am not sure of having elucidated. This last line, which recurs in each of these verses (12-16), is "*de ni syra-yis drang-du rung.*"

19.

They who delight in the law taught by the elect, who follow it in body and speech, who delight in the society of the patient, who control their senses, they will obtain the reward of hearing and of understanding.

Chapter on " The Hearer," the Twenty-second.

XXIII.

SELF (ATMA).

1.

LEARN what has been well explained, associate only with Çramanas,[1] (live) in seclusion and with only a single mat, and thy mind will be at rest.

2.

He who has but a single mat, one resting-place (the earth?), who is without indolence, who dwells alone in a forest, he will learn to control himself.

3 (103).

He who conquers a thousand times a thousand men in battle, a greater conqueror than he is he who conquers himself.[2]

4 (104).

He who by continual control has conquered himself has by this one conquest gained so great a victory that that over the rest of mankind could not add to it.

5 (105).

The Bhixu who has conquered through knowledge,

---

[1] *Bsñen-bkur,* "to reverence;" but P. explains it here by "to associate only with virtuous persons (Kalyanamitra)."

[2] On hearing of the great victories of Prasenajit, who had been surnamed the Victorious, Bhagavat spoke verses 3, 4, 5.—P.

Mâra and Brahmâ cannot defeat him, nor can a Deva or a Gandharva.[1]

6 (158).

If one in the first place has done that which is right, he can afterwards discipline others to be like himself; if one in the first place has done that which is right, afterwards the wise man and those he shall have disciplined [2] will be free from suffering.[3]

7.

If a man make others as he has made himself, then, being subdued and at rest, he can educate others to be happy.

8 (159).

If a man would make others as he has made himself, ah! let yourself be well subdued, for it is difficult to subdue one's self.

9 (166).

One must give up what is beneficial to the multitude for what is for one's own good; when one has found that which is so greatly beneficial to himself, let him make his own welfare his chief concern.[4]

10.

Self is the lord of self;[5] what other lord could there

---

[1] Mâra, i.e., the lord of the region of desires; Brahmâ, i.e., the lord of all the regions of the universe; Deva, i.e., they who are still in the regions of desire, which the Bhixu has left behind; Gandharva, i.e., the joyous, who play music, &c.—P.

[2] Hdul-tso mkhas-pa. I am not quite sure that tso is correct, but this is evidently the sense of the phrase. P. says, "By causing others to enter the right way he and others will not suffer."

[3] There was an old man in Çravasti who was in the habit of jesting, joking, and talking nonsense with the Brahmans and householders who passed by, and who did insolently scoff to Brahmans and householders about the teaching of the Dharma. Bhagavat (on hearing him) spoke these three (6, 7, 8) verses.—P.

[4] A Bhixu at Çravasti, who had heard but very little of the law, was so greatly delighted, that he would enter the town every now and then (ñung-du ñung-du) to teach the Brahmans and householders. Bhagavat spoke this verse to prevent him doing this.—P.

[5] Bhagavat spoke these ten verses (10–14) for the following reason: He had entered a vihâra where he saw a Bhixu very ill, who had been

be? The wise man who has become master of himself finds great profit.

11.

Self is the lord of self; what other lord could there be? The wise man who has become master of himself finds the law.[1]

12.

Self is the lord of self; what other lord could there be? The wise man who has become master of himself finds what is glorious.

13.

Self is the lord of self; what other lord could there be? The wise man who has become master of himself finds happiness.

14.

Self is the lord of self; what other lord could there be? The wise man who has become master of himself finds how to reach felicity.

15.

Self is the lord of self; what other lord could there be? The wise man who has become master of himself will find joy for a long time in heaven.

16.

Self is the lord of self; what other lord could there be? The wise man who has become master of himself is a beacon to his relatives.

---

left for a whole week lying in the midst of his excrements unattended. He was a naturally violent man, and he had loudly cursed, saying that the priests (*tsangs-pa tsungs par spyod-pa rnams*) showed him no respect. Therefore the Bhixus had left him. Drawing nigh (Bhagavat) said, "Bhixus, why do you not attend on your upâdhyâya who is ill? Do not masters and disciples wait on each other when ill? Besides, is he not your upâdhyâya?" "He is not our master," they answered. See vol. lxxii. fol. 61.

[1] The law that frees him of worldly existence, which prevents him returning.—P. Or, "he finds the essential thing."

17.

Self is the lord of self; what other lord could there be? He who has become master of himself will find no pain in the midst of sorrow.[1]

18.

Self is the lord of self; what other lord could there be? He who has become master of himself cuts off all bonds.

19.

Self is the lord of self; what other lord could there be? He who has become master of himself casts off all evil births.

20 (160).

Self is the lord of self; what other lord could there be? He who has become master of himself finds a patron[2] in himself.

21.

Self is the lord of self; what other lord could there be? He who becomes master of himself draws nigh unto nirvâṇa itself (or unto the real destruction of sorrow).[3]

Chapter on " The Self," the Twenty-third.

---

[1] He will feel no pain although he lives in the regions of desire, &c.—P. This and preceding verse seem to be another version of xvi. 11, 12.

[2] *Myon* is here explained by "what is useful to himself."—P.

[3] This verse was addressed to two Bhixus by the name of Dakshana (?). Nirvâṇa is said to be the destruction of the skandhas, escape from the orb of transmigration.—P.

XXIV.

NUMBERS (OR COMPARISONS).

1 (100).

It is better to speak one word of sense which brings one nigh unto peace, than to recite a hundred gâthâs which are without sense.

2 (102).

It is better to speak one word of the law which brings one nigh unto peace, than to recite a hundred gâthâs which are not of the law.

3 (110).

He who lives a hundred years violating all his vows, a life of one single day is better if one observes all his vows.

4 (112).

He who lives a hundred years in laziness and slothfulness, a life of one single day is better if one exerts oneself to zealous application.

5 (111).

He who lives a hundred years, his mind without aim or object, a life of one single day is better if one is wise and well composed.

6 (113).

He who lives a hundred years without perceiving birth and dissolution, a life of one single day is better if one perceives birth and dissolution.

7.

He who lives a hundred years without perceiving the ending of perception (vedanâ),[1] a life of one single day is better if one perceives the ending of perception.

8.

He who lives a hundred years without perceiving the end of sin (âsrava), a life of one single day is better if one perceives the end of sin.

9 (114).

He who lives a hundred years without perceiving the unchanging place,[2] a life of one single day is better if one perceives the unchanging place (nirvâṇa).

10.

He who lives a hundred years without knowing the ideal knowledge that is hard (to arrive at),[3] a life of one single day is better if one knows the ideal knowledge that is hard (to arrive at).

11.

He who lives a hundred years without perceiving what is most exalted,[4] a life of one single day is better if one perceives what is most exalted.

12.

He who lives a hundred years without perceiving the perfection of the holy (law), a life of one single day is

---

[1] Who does not learn how to free himself from the passions proceeding from the two regions of form.—P.

[2] *Go-hphang mi-gyo;* compare the Pâli, *amatam padam. Mi-gyo,* "unchanging," seems here to be used in the same way as *amatam* for "nirvâṇa," *i.e.,* it is unchangeable because there is neither birth nor death. See Childers, s.v. "Amata." As to *go-hphang,* the lexicons translate it by rank, degree, &c., and possibly by extension, "place," like *pada.* Any other translation of this word would hardly convey the idea of the original. P. explains it by "the real immortal, nirvâṇa."

[3] Having left the senses behind to comprehend by the yoga.—P.

[4] The root of virtue.—P. But this explanation is inadmissible. See note 5, p. 104.

better if one perceives the perfection of the holy (law, *i.e.*, nirvâṇa).¹

13.

He who lives a hundred years without perceiving the perfect cessation of death, a life of one single day is better if one perceives the perfect cessation of death.

14.

He who lives a hundred years without perceiving the most perfect amrita,² a life of one single day is better if one perceives the most perfect amrita.

15.

He who lives a hundred years without perceiving perfect passionlessness,³ a life of one single day is better if one perceives perfect passionlessness.

16.

He who lives a hundred years without perceiving the perfect absence of passion,⁴ a life of one single day is better if one perceives the perfect absence of passion (raga).⁵

17 (107).

If a man live for a hundred years in a forest, wholly

---

¹ This verse is repeated in the text of the Bkah-hgyur and in that of the Bstan-hgyur. The Commentary, however, reads *ma-byas* in verse 12, and *dam-pa* in the following. *Ma-byas*, "the unmade," free from cause and effect, a qualification of nirvâṇa. According to this arrangement there is an extra verse, and the 12 of the text of the Bkah-hgyur becomes 12b.

² Comp. *amata* as used in Pâli for "nectar," and an epithet of nirvâṇa. This appears to be the meaning of this verse. P. says, "The destruction of fear, because there is no death."

³ *Rdul-med go-hphang*, the destruction of ignorance, selfishness, &c.—P.

⁴ Separation from sin and from the passions of the regions of desire. —P.

⁵ "Destruction of perceptions, &c. (see verse 7, *et seq.*), are all spoken about nirvâṇa."—P. That is to say, that from verse 7 to 17 all the perfections (*go-hphang*) mentioned are indicative of the happiness of nirvâṇa.

relying on the fire [1] (Agni), and if he but for one single moment pays homage to a man who meditates on the self, this homage is greater than sacrifices for a hundred years.

18.

He who month after month eats his food with a tip (of a blade) of kuça grass, is not worth the sixteenth part of him who has faith in the Buddha.

19 (70).

He who month after month eats his food with a tip (of a blade) of kuça grass, is not worth the sixteenth part of him who has faith in the holy law.

20.

He who month after month eats his food with a tip (of a blade) of kuça grass, is not worth the sixteenth part of him who has faith in the church (Sangha).

21.

He who month after month eats his food with a tip (of a blade) of kuça grass, is not worth the sixteenth part of him who is merciful to sentient creatures.[2]

22.

He who month after month eats his food with a tip (of a blade) of kuça grass, is not worth the sixteenth part of him who is merciful to animated creatures.[3]

23.

He who month after month eats his food with a tip

---

[1] The Commentary mentions three kinds of fires, which it calls *garhavati*, *ahavani*, and *dakshana*, to which the fire-worshippers successively say *bhu*, *bhu bho*, and *sva*. See Commentary, vol. lxxii. fol. 67a.

[2] *Sems-chan-rnams*, "having a mind."

[3] *Srog-tchags-rnams*. The Maitri-bhavana Sûtra (Mdo xxx. f. 575, 576a), also in the Pâli Pitaka, has some quite pretty verses on the reward of mercy.

(of a blade) of kuça grass, is not worth the sixteenth part of him who is merciful to beings (bhuta).[1]

24.

He who month after month eats his food with the tip (of a blade) of kuça grass, is not worth the sixteenth part of him who seeks to show kindness.

25.

He who month after month eats his food with the tip (of a blade) of kuça grass, is not worth the sixteenth part of him who explains well the holy law.

26.

He who for a hundred years makes a thousand sacrifices[2] each month, is not worth the sixteenth part of him who has faith in the Buddha.

27.

He who for a hundred years makes a thousand sacrifices each month, is not worth the sixteenth part of him who has faith in the holy law.

28.

He who for a hundred years makes a thousand sacrifices each month, is not worth the sixteenth part of him who has faith in the church (Sangha).

29.

He who for a hundred years makes a thousand sacrifices each month, is not worth the sixteenth part of him who is merciful to sentient creatures.

30.

He who for a hundred years makes a thousand sacrifices

---

[1] *Hbyung-po-rnams*, i.e., "who inhale breath."—P.

[2] According to some commentators, this means "who offers a thousand karshapanas.—P.

each month, is not worth the sixteenth part of him who is merciful to animated creatures.

31.

He who for a hundred years makes a thousand sacrifices each month, is not worth the sixteenth part of him who is merciful to beings (bhuta).

32.

He who for a hundred years makes a thousand sacrifices each month, is not worth the sixteenth part of him who seeks to show kindness.

33.

He who for a hundred years makes a thousand sacrifices each month, is not worth the sixteenth part of him who explains well the holy law.

34 (108).

No matter what sacrifice a man may offer in this world to acquire merit, it is not worth the quarter of doing homage to one who has a quieted and upright mind.

Chapter on "Numbers," the Twenty-fourth.

BOOK III.

Book III.

XXV.

FRIENDSHIP.

1.

THE wise man should not know him who is without faith, who is avaricious, who stirs up strife, and who slanders; he should not associate with the wicked.[1]

2.

The wise man should have as his friends those who have faith, who speak pleasingly, who are attentive, virtuous, and wise; he should associate with the best of men.

3 (78).

Do not keep sinful persons as associates, stay not with the wicked; keep virtuous friends, stay with righteous men. If one associates with such as these, he becomes not sinful, but righteous.[2]

4.

Associate with them who have listened much, retained much, who reflect, who have faith and wisdom; if one

---

[1] At Çravasti, on the one side of Bhagavat were Devâdatta, Kaṭamorakatishya, &c., and on the other Çariputra and all those who had cast off passions. Seeing the contempt which the Brahmans and householders showed Devâdatta, and the homages they offered the venerable Çariputra, (Bhagavat) spoke these three verses (1, 2, 3).—P.

[2] Comp. Kalyâna-mitra sevana Sûtra, Mdo xxv.; Feer, Textes tirés du Kandjour, liv. iv. pp. 10, 11.

but hearken here to the pleasing words (of these men), he will attain that which surpasses everything.[1]

5.

He who associates with what is low is contaminated by (their) sinfulness; he who associates with what is entirely fallen is held down to earth;[2] associating with what is best brings one to righteousness. Keep then to those who will raise you to excellence.

6.

If one associates with those best of men who are virtuous, dispassionate, who have the best of knowledge, though one be good,[3] one will arrive at still greater excellence.

7.

It is with him who associates with the sinful as with the sweet kuça grass in which a man wrapped up some decayed fish; the kuça also became decayed.

8.

It is with him who associates with the virtuous as with the palâça leaves[4] in which a man wrapped up some incense (tagara); the leaves also became scented.[5]

---

[1] *Ring-po-nas kyang khyad-par thob-par-hgyur.* The Commentary explains this by "he will obtain the highest understanding" (*utrayanai rtogs-pa*).

[2] *Thad-kar bab-pa bsten-pas so-na gnas,* i.e., associating with sinners, he will not be able to escape transmigration. I have translated *so-na* as if it were *sa-na*. The change of the *a* into *o* is possible, according to M. Jäschke. See s.v. "So," ii. p. 578.

[3] *Gtso-bo-bas kyang tches gtsor hgyur,* which may also be rendered, "he will become more perfect than the perfect (with whom he is associating)."

[4] *Pa-la-shai lo-ma,* the *Butea frondosa.* See Childers, s.v. "Palâso."

[5] Compare Dsang-blun, p. 110: "When tsampaka-flowers are pressed together with rape-seed, does not the oil retain the sweet odour of the flowers?" Comp. Stan. Julien, Avadânas, ii. pp. 32–34; (extract from the "Fa-yu-pi-yu King") Beal, Romantic Legend, p. 376; and Dham., p. 66.

9.

If those who are not wicked associate with the wicked, there arises an inclination to do evil, which will grow into open acts of wickedness: by associating with those with whom one ought not to associate, one becomes sinful through their sinfulness.[1]

10.

As when an arrow has been dipped in poison, even where the poison has not come in contact with it, it is poisonous, so are those who are clothed in sin, that source of terror: keep not wicked friends.

11.

As are one's associates, as is what one holds fast to, so will one become in a short while: examine well, then, whom you associate with, as you would a basket of fruit.

12.

Not associating with the unrighteous, the wise man associates with the righteous; by following this road the Bhixu[2] will find the end of misery.

13 (64).

If a fool for the whole of his life be associated with a wise man, he will no more perceive the law than does a spoon the taste of soup.

14 (65).

If an intelligent man be associated for an instant with a wise man, he will perceive the law as does the tongue the taste of soup.

---

[1] Bhagavat spoke verses 9-12 to King Adjatasatru, who was associating with evil friends (Devâdatta), and caused him to repent.—P. This cannot stand comparison with Menander's celebrated "Evil communications corrupt good manners."

[2] He who has cast off the kleças.—P. "End of misery," *i.e.*, end of the three evil ways (inferior births).—P.

15.

If a fool for the whole of his life be associated with a wise man, as he has no eyes he will not perceive the law.

16.

If an intelligent man be only for an instant associated with a wise man, he, having eyes, will perceive the law.

17.

If a fool for the whole of his life be associated with a wise man, he will not understand the law taught by the perfect Buddha.

18.

If an intelligent man be only associated for an instant with a wise man, he will understand the law taught by the perfect Buddha.

19.

A single significant word suffices for him who is wise; all the teaching of the Buddha would not suffice for the fool.

20.

He who is intelligent will with one word know a hundred; the fool with a thousand words will not know a single one.

21.

The wise man cares not for fools, he makes not his friends of fools; for he who is fond of the society of fools is led down to hell.[1]

22 (63).

If a fool says, "I am a fool," he is wise in that knowledge; but the fool who thinks himself a wise man, he is called "a fool" (indeed).

---

[1] The two sons of a rich merchant had made evil-doers their friends, and had been put to death by King Adjatasatru for having committed adultery.—P.

23.

When the fool doth praise and when the wise man doth scorn; the scorn of the wise man is just, but improper is the praise of the fool.[1]

24 (207).

He who associates with a fool is in misery, as if he were with an enemy;[2] one ought not to associate with fools, neither ought one to listen to or see them; associating with the steadfast is happiness, like meeting again one's kinsfolk.

25 (208).

Therefore, as the moon keeps to the path of the constellations, so likewise keep (only) with them who are steadfast, erudite, who know what is best, virtuous, with the manners of the elect (Ariyas), pre-eminent, kind, and intelligent.

Chapter on Friendship, the Twenty-fifth.

---

[1] Spoken on account of Devâdatta's reformation.
[2] "Who is ready to strike him with a sword."—P.

XXVI.

NIRVÂNA.

1.

The Bhixu who concentrates within himself all the faculties of his mind as the tortoise draws its body into its shell,[1] attached to nothing, injuring no one, does naught to impede (the attaining of) nirvâna.[2]

2 (184).

Patience is the greatest penance; patience, the Buddha says, is the greatest nirvâna: he who is a priest and who injures others, who harms others, is not a Çramana (lit. one who practises virtue).[3]

3 (133).

Use no harsh words, for as one has been spoken to so will he answer; quarrelsome words bring sorrow, they receive their punishment.

4.

He who sends forth (evil-sounding words) like a bronze vase that has been struck, will suffer for a long time, wandering about from birth to old age.

---

[1] To protect itself from the fox (or otter?) who wanted to devour him.—P.

[2] Comp. Beal, *loc. cit.*, p. 73, and Stan. Julien, Avadânas, i. p. 141, *et seq.*; also Bhagavadgitâ, ii. 58, *Yada sanharate tchayam kurmo*, &c., "If, as the tortoise draws in all its limbs, he abstracts his senses from sensible objects, in him wisdom is established."

[3] Comp. Pratimoxa Sûtra, 1; Mel. Asiat., viii. pp. 590 and 593; Beal, Catena, p. 158, where it is taken from the Chinese Pratimoxa.

5 (134).

He who does not send forth (evil-sounding words) like a bronze vase that has not been struck, occasioning no quarrels, he will find nirvâṇa.

6 (204).

Absence of disease is the best of possessions, contentedness the best of riches, a true friend the best of friends, nirvâṇa the greatest happiness.

7 (203).

All compound things (sanskâra) the greatest of pains, hunger the worst of diseases; if one has found this out, he has found the highest nirvâṇa.

8.

Let one but consider the way to attain happiness and the way to go to perdition, and when he has thus formed an idea of sin, it will not be long ere he reaches nirvâṇa.

9.

The way to attain happiness proceeds from a cause; the way to go to perdition has its cause; the way to nirvâṇa has its cause; they all have a cause.

10.

The deer go chiefly to the woods, the birds fly into the air; he who devotes himself to the law goes to the nirvâṇa of the Arhat.[1]

11.

He who strives but feebly, who has little intelligence and no learning, will not find nirvâṇa, that destruction of all bonds.

---

[1] *Dyra-bchom mga-ngan*, &c. He who has conquered the enemy (*dyra-bchom*) sin, obtains the nirvâṇa of the destruction of the skandhas.—P. Or, "the Arhat goes to nirvâṇa," a more natural translation.

12 (369).

The pilot of this boat makes it light; so if you cast away hatred and passions, you will reach nirvâna.[1]

13.

If what has formerly been born is not born, there will be produced that which is not born (the elementary); that which is not born (the elementary) not producing (compound things), there is an end to production itself.[2]

14.

He who perceives what is difficult to see (suffering), and who heeds not uncertain happiness,[3] who understands the truth and has knowledge, who sees the nothingness of desires (trichnâ) and (worldly) joy, he who is like unto this has put an end to suffering.

15.

Having cast off desires (trichnâ), having cast away passions, (I am) like unto a dried-up lake that flows no more; he who is like unto this puts an end to suffering.[4]

---

[1] Bhagavat was going in the summer-time to Varanâsi, and arriving on the shore of the Ganges, a boatman invited him into his boat. So he and his disciples entered into it; but it filling with water, the boatman said to the other men in the boat, "Bail it out (*phyogs-shig*), so that the boat may not sink."—P. Comp. Beal, Romantic Legend, p. 289.

[2] Bhagavat was at Uruvilva a short time after having attained perfect enlightenment, when he thought: "Through the production of what thing have I been brought into this existence, and by the suppression of what will I be relieved of it? The elementary is perfectly free, therefore if there is no birth and no not birth, birth will not be." Then he said, &c. —P. Comp. Lalita Vistara, chap.

xxii. p. 331, *et seq.*, of M. Foucaux's translation.

[3] *Mtha-med bder mi mthong*. The commentator explains *mtha-med* by *hdir mthai sgra ni nges-pai tsig-go*. Not being given to trichnâ, which causes suffering (the second truth), he consequently knows the cessation of suffering, or the third truth. I have endeavoured to follow the Commentary in translating this verse, the first part of which is unintelligible without its assistance, and in which I suspect errors.

[4] Bhagavat was at Uruvilva a short time after having attained perfect enlightenment, and was receiving the homages of a great concourse of devas. Some of them asserted that he was a perfect Buddha, others said he was not, some were uncertain. Bhagavat, knowing their minds, rose up in the air to the height of seven

NIRVANA.   119

16.

He whose sensations (vedana) have become cool, whose perceptions (sandjâ) are suppressed, whose being (sanskâra) is at rest, whose consciousness (viññana) has disappeared; he who is like unto this puts an end to suffering.[1]

17.

He who has perceived what ought to be seen, who has heard what ought to be listened to, who has understood what ought to be understood, who knows perfectly what ought to be known perfectly; he who is like this puts an end to suffering: he who only longs for the thing which ought to be longed for (*i.e.*, to be at rest), he who is like unto this puts an end to suffering.

18.

He who delights not in what is tangible, who is at peace, who casts off every passion; he who is like unto this puts an end to suffering.

19.

From the source (ignorance)[2] springs the commission

---

tala (trees), and pronounced this solemn utterance (udâna udânesi). — P. Comp. Lalita Vistara, p. 336 (trans.)

[1] This is said to teach the four truths. The four attributes alluded to are four of the skandhas. "Bhagavat was in the Aduma (Âtumâ) country, as was also a Rischi from Aduma called Keneya (Keniya). Bhagavat, while resting at noon on the bank of a gently flowing brook, thought, 'Who is there in the world to whom I can impart the fourfold protecting law?' and then he perceived that the Rischi Keniya could be converted with but little trouble," &c. Comp. Mahâvagga, vi. 36, where Keniya is called a *jatila*, "an ascetic wearing long, matted hair." On "Âtumâ," see Mahâvagga, vi. 37.

According to the Commentary, ver. 16 ought to be placed after 17.

[2] *Rten-pa*, which the Commentary explains by saying, "that is, ignorance, which is the root of existence." This verse seems to be an unusual form of the theory of the twelve Nidânas. Its origin is this:—A Brahman by the name of Utakatarga, who knew all the theories (sidhanta) of the three Vedas, of the Pradjnâparamita, of Agni (?), came nigh unto Bhagavat, and asked him, "Çramana Gautama, some philosophers (*mu-stegs*) contend that this world being everlasting (*ther-zug*), there is no getting free of it; others say that on dying one goes not to another world, and that, according to the Vedas, there is no transmigration. What say you to this, Gautama, I pray you?"—P.

(of sins); from the commission springs the binding (to their consequences); from the binding springs that which is not to be removed (transmigration); from that which is not to be removed springs going and coming; from going and coming springs suffering another death; from having to suffer another death springs another birth, and old age, disease, death, sorrow, misery, affliction, unhappiness, disagreeabilities [1] are created; and in this manner does one bring on oneself a great amount of suffering.[2]

20.

There being no source (ignorance), there is no commission; there being no commission (of sins), there is no binding to (their consequences); there being no binding, there is not that which is not to be removed; there not being that which is not to be removed, there is no going and coming; there being no going and coming, there is no suffering another death; there being no suffering another death, there is not another birth, and old age, disease, death, sorrow, misery, affliction, unhappiness, disagreeabilities are stopped; and in this way one puts an end to a great amount of suffering.

21.

Bhixus, the uncreated, the invisible, the unmade, the elementary, the unproduced, exist (as well as) the created, the visible, the made, the conceivable, the compound, the produced; and there is an uninterrupted connection between the two.[3]

---

[1] Such as cold, heat, insects, flies (*sha-shrang*), wind.—P.

[2] From this paragraph to No. 29 the text is in prose.

[3] A great many Bhixus were gathered together in a resting-house, and were systematising nirvâṇa and the law of connection between cause and effect, as also on what was to be looked for in nirvâṇa, but they were in some uncertainty. Bhagavat, who had heard them, then spoke these words.—P. The five first terms, we are also told, are the five portions (*tcha*) or felicities (*mthun*) of being delivered of all attachments. See Commentary, vol. lxxii. fol. 92. They represent the state of one who has reached the nirvâṇa of the destruction of the elements of existence.

22.

Bhixus, if the uncreated, the invisible, the unmade, the elementary, the unproduced was nonentity,[1] I could not say that the result of their connection from cause to effect with the created, the visible, the made, the compound, the conceivable was final emancipation.[2]

23.

Bhixus, it is because of the real existence of the uncreated, the invisible, the elementary, the unproduced that I say that the result of their connection from cause to effect[3] with the created, the visible, the made, the compound, the conceivable is final emancipation.

24.

The impermanency of the created, the visible, the made, the produced, the compound, the great torment of subjection to old age, death, and ignorance, what proceeds from the cause of eating;[4] (all this) is destroyed, and there is found no delight in it; this is the essential feature of final emancipation. Then there will be no doubts and scruples; all sources of suffering will be stopped,[5] and one will have the happiness of the peace of the sanskâra.[6]

---

[1] "If nirvâṇa was annihilation." —P.

[2] *Nges-par-hbyung.* This term is generally used for *niryanika* (Pâli *niyyaniko*), "final emancipation." See Jäschke, s.v. "Nges-pa." The Commentary explains it by "that which really exists, consequently the condition (bhava, *dngos*) of the other world is not nothingness. All conditions (*dngos*) are related, and it cannot be conceived that there is one that is isolated: light is (connected) with darkness, heat with cold, &c. . . . What, then, is nirvâṇa? It is the end of suffering and final emancipation (*nges-hbyung*) and life (*dus*) without end." See Commentary, vol. lxxii. fol. 93.

[3] *Rten-ching hbrel-bar hbyung,* "the coming to pass in continuous connection." Jäschke, s.v. "Rten." See on the twelve Nidânas, Burnouf, Intr. à l'Hist. du Buddh. Indien, p. 485, *et seq.*

[4] "When the wise man has examined the cause of eating, he enters the priesthood and is dependent on another (thing?). Beings exist by eating; without eating there would be no existence. Food is the exciting cause of suffering, the origin of suffering.—P.

[5] The five skandhas.—P.

[6] This is the highest happiness of nirvâṇa.—P. This is about as explicit a description of the state of parinirvâṇa (*anupadisesanibbâna*) as can be found in the Tibetan canon.

25.

Bhixus,[1] it (nirvâṇa) is neither in earth, or in water, fire, or wind.[2]

26.

It (nirvâṇa) is not in a spiritual state (âyatana) in the immensity of space, nor in a spiritual state of infinite wisdom, nor in a spiritual state in the region of nothing, nor in a spiritual state in the region where there is no conception (and) where there is not no (conception);[3] it is not in this world or in another world; it is not in either the sun or the moon: these (ideas) are not, I assert, the correct conception (of it).

27.

Bhixus, as I say it does not exist with going and coming, it is what is not existence;[4] as I do not say it exists where there is death, it is not to be born: this then is the end of suffering.[5]

28.

It (nirvâṇa) does not exist in either earth, water, fire, or wind;[6] in it white (and the other colours) are not

---

[1] Bhagavat was residing in a forest, and was teaching the Bhixus a proper belief in nirvâṇa. Then the Bhixus thought, "What, then, is it?" But he, understanding their thoughts, said, "It is emancipation from all suffering; it is the knowledge of the real nature (bhava, dngos) of all things; it is as if a man held an amalaka (fruit) in his hand; it is the possession of the knowledge to stop, &c. This is what you must believe; this is what I teach."—P.

[2] These belong to the regions of desire and of form, and they, I teach, do not contain it (nirvâṇa). In these (regions) there exists both pleasure and pain; like a garland of tchandana or other flowers, which have also in them (either) poison or thorns, so is it with these two regions.—P.

[3] These appertain to the region without form.—P. Wassilieff, Buddhisme, p. 249, mentions these four âyatanas: "The four kinds of âyatana are nothing else than the four kinds of samapatti or contemplation, which correspond with the invisible world." See also note 4, p. 242 of the same work. This and preceding paragraph are evidently an adaptation of a passage of the Brahmajâla Sûtra. See Grimblot, Sept Suttas Palis, p. 43, and Mdo, xxx. f. 128b.

[4] Gnas-par ma-yin-no. The Commentary explains the first word by saying gnas-pai gnas skabs, "a condition, state of being."

[5] This is complete nirvâṇa, the cessation (lit. calm) of all harm.—P.

[6] This verse is to summarise the teaching of the three preceding verses. —P.

visible;[1] in it there is not even darkness; in it the moon does not shine, nor does the sun send forth its rays.

29.

He who is a Muni[2] and a Brâhmana, and who is consequently wise, is delivered from the material (rûpa) and the immaterial (arûpa), and from all kinds of suffering.[3]

30.

He who has reached the end[4] and is without fear, is without pride and without sin; having left behind the pains of existence, he has a body for the last time.

31.

This is the chief (beatitude) of those who have reached the end, perfect and unsurpassable peace (amatam padam), the destruction of all characteristics, the perfection of perfect purity, the annihilation of death.

32.

The Muni having cast off the sanskâra of existence (and also) like and unlike, by delighting in perfect composure he has broken the shell of the egg of existence and goes out (of the world).[5]

---

[1] "For it is the elementary" in which colours cannot exist (?). "White and darkness mean day and night."—P. It would seem, according to P., that we ought to translate "there is not even darkness, for the moon," &c.; but this is not quite in accordance with the text.

[2] According to P., this term may either mean an Arhat or one who has found out nirvâna. Brâhmana means one who has cast off passions.

[3] The versified part recommences with this udâna.

[4] The Ayuchmat Kshepaka was living in the complete seclusion of a forest, and having through earnestness obtained the fruit of arhatship, he was savouring the bliss of perfect freedom. Verses 30 and 31 were spoken of him.—P.

[5] Bhagavat spoke this verse to Ananda while at Vaisali. As when in a hen's egg the body has matured (the chick) breaks the shell with its beak and having crushed it, comes out, so in like manner Bhagavat, having destroyed sins by his perfect knowledge of their nature and of the nature of sinfulness, has entered into nirvâna. The happiness of nirvâna eclipses all happinesses. That is what this teaches.—P. This consequently alludes to the nirvâna which forms part of the condition of the Arhat while still in life—Kilesanibbâna. See Childers, s.v. "Nibbâna," p. 266, et seq.

33 (354).

The greatest of gifts is the gift of the law; the greatest of delights is delight in the law; the greatest of strengths is the strength of patience; the greatest happiness is the destruction of desire (trichnâ).[1]

Chapter on Nirvâṇa, the Twenty-sixth.

---

[1] Spoken in answer to four questions of a deva.—P. I follow the Commentary in translating "delight in the law;" the text has *tchos-kyi dyah*. See on the use of *kyi* instead of *la*, Foucaux, Gram. Tib., p. 92.

XXVII.

SIGHT.

1 (252).

It is easier to see the faults of others than those of oneself; the faults of others are easily seen, for they are sifted like chaff, but one's own faults are difficult to see. It is like the cheat who shows the dice (of his adversary) and hides his own, calling attention to the shortcomings of the other (player), and continually thinking of accusing him; he is far from seeing what is right (dharma), and greatly increases his unhappy lot.[1]

2 (244).

Life is easy for an impudent, thieving, boasting fellow, with filthy (instincts?) like a crow,[2] who leads a life of sinfulness and impudicity.

3 (245).

Life is hard for the man who is always seeking what is pure, who is disinterested, temperate, chaste, and modest.

4 (174).

This world is in darkness; few there are who have

---

[1] *Gyon-phyogs*, which the Commentary explains by "disgraceful;" he adds to his natural wickedness.

[2] *Mi-gtsang las ldan kha lta-bu*. The Pâli version is *kâkasûrena*, "a crow hero." I prefer the Tibetan.

spiritual insight,[1] and who, like birds escaped from a net, go to enjoy the heavens.

5.

The fool who is held in bondage by his body is wrapped in darkness; they who covet worldly goods consider all other things in this same (sinful) way.[2]

6.

Some think sentient beings are their own creators, some think that another (Isvara, &c.) made them; they who take as the truth what is not the truth can see nothing at all; not seeing that they are not even unanimous on this point,[3] they cannot perceive misery.

7.

It enters not the mind of those beings who seek the pleasures of the senses that the misery they have until then seen (brought on themselves) is their own work; they do not understand that other like deeds will bring (misery also with them).

8.

Those beings who are selfish, fond of selfishness, held in the bonds of selfishness, who are given to controversial opinions,[4] will not escape from the orb of transmigration.

---

[1] *Lhag-mthong-ldan* (in Pâli *vipassanâ*), "produced by the successful exercise of ecstatic meditation, and is an attribute of arhatship." Childers, s.v.; Spence Hardy, Manual of Buddhism, p. 232, *et passim*.

[2] He considers as despicable the qualities necessary for the attainment of happiness; (cupidity) is the foundation of all wickedness. He is like a wild beast, a piçâtcha, a famished beast, a wolf after other men's possessions.—P.

[3] *De ni hyas-kyang mi-mthong dsing*. I translate *hyas* by "not unanimous," in accordance with the Commentary, which says *hyas-kyang*, that is, "that is thus considered by only one." This phrase, however, is very obscure. It seems to imply that they who have such a very slight idea of the real nature of the world cannot, of course, perceive the misery of life and the cause of misery.

[4] Who are fond of the sixty-two opinions (*lta*).—P. That is to say, the sixty-two heterodox opinions discussed in the Brahmajâla Sûtra.

9.

Know that the (births) that one has been subject to, and those that he will be subject to, all of these are wrapped in sinfulness (râga); they are subject to decay.[1]

10.

There are those who practise morality, the precepts, good behaviour, who lead a life of holiness (brahmachariya), and there is an extreme which is to devote oneself to asceticism.[2]

11.

And there is another extreme in which they say: "Desires are pure; though one has desires he is virtuous; desires are to be indulged in; desires have nothing sinful in them." These men are swallowed up by their desires.[3] (The followers of) both these extreme (theories), frequenting mostly burial-places, are called "frequenters of burial-places" (sosâniko).[4]

12.

Neither of these extremes see (the cause of suffering), so part of them are filled with desires, and part of them are wildly running about;[5] they who can see perceive how full of desires they are, and how they run about.

---

[1] A Bhixu having returned to Bhagavat after the rainy season, the Blessed One asked him, "Bhixu, where have you passed the summer?" "I have passed it in the Himavat mountains." "What did you see marvellous, O Bhixu?" He answered Bhagavat, "I saw Rischis coming from and going to heaven; I was filled with delight, and longed to know when I would be like them."—P.

[2] I consider this and the following phrase as being a version of the two extremes mentioned in the sermon of Benares (Dharma çakra pravartana Sûtra). My translation is conjectural; the general sense, however, is quite clear.

[3] Like a fly falling in the milk (it is enjoying).—P.

[4] I do not understand the latter part of this verse; the Commentary only says that "the *dur-khrod-hphel-ba* (sosâniko?) with unenlightened mind sees not and cannot understand." On the practice of frequenting burial-places, to reflect on the impermanency of the body, which is one of the thirteen dhutanga precepts, see Burnouf, Introd. à l'Hist. Bud., p. 308, *et seq.*

[5] "*Mngon-par rgyug-par-byed.*" That is to say, going after desires even to a great distance, to enjoy the region of form, &c.—P. "Filled with desires" alludes to those who devote themselves to outward acts of penance.

13.

They who can see, perceive that if these two extremes could but see, they would give up desires and cease running (after them); so they have no desires, and do not run about (after them). As they do not thus, as they think not thus (*i.e.*, as the two extremes), as they are not held in this way, they have found the end of suffering.

14 (170).

He who looks on the world as a bubble, who considers it as a mirage, the king of death will not see him.[1]

15.

He who looks on the body as a bubble, who considers it as a mirage, the king of death will not see him.

16 (171).

Look always at this body as at a beautiful royal chariot; the fool delights in it, the wise man has no fondness for it.[2]

17.

Look always at this body as at a beautiful royal chariot; the fool is deceived by it, the wise man is not deceived by it.

18.

Look always at this body as at a beautiful royal chariot; the fool is brought low through it, like an old elephant sunk in the mud.

19.

Look always at this body as sick and subject to decay, as a wounded man, as changing and impermanent.

---

[1] "He will become an Arhat."—P.

[2] The eight following verses (16-23) were spoken of Ayuchmat Râstrapâla, who, having acquired the perfect manners of the priesthood, went to Sthulakoshtha (*sic*) for the sake of his parents, &c.—P. See this episode in Dulva, ii. fol. 214, *et seq.*

20.

Look at this body, ornamented with jewels, bracelets, and ear-rings, as diseased and subject to decay, as changing and impermanent.

21.

The fool in his stupidity adorns his curls, paints his eyes with collyr, and seeks not after the other world.

22.

The fool in his stupidity paints (his body) with colours,[1] covers with jewels this corrupt body,[2] and seeks not after the other world.

23.

The fool in his stupidity anoints this body with perfumes, rubs his feet with gerika,[3] and seeks not after the other world.

24.

He who is entirely devoted to desires, and who sees not the sinfulness of his devotion, is unable through his devotion to desires to cross the wide and eternal stream.

25.

He who has commenced by casting off the principal desires, and finally all of them, who looks neither to the I or the mine, crosses the until then impassable stream, and finishes with existence.

---

[1] *Mig-sman-gis.* "A variety of powders similar in colour to antimony (?) (*mthing-shun*)." It here means that patterns are drawn on the individual to beautify his or her person.

[2] "With strings of gold on the head, strings of pearls round the neck, bracelets round the wrists and feet, &c."—P.

[3] *Btsag-pa.* "Made of *li-khri* (minium) *sen-rtsi* (ochre?) &c." According to M. Jäschke, *btsag* means "red ochre;" according to Childers, "red chalk."

26 (344).

He who having freed himself of the forest,[1] being without the forest, runs to the forest, though he has freed himself of it; look at that miserable man who gives up freedom for bondage!

27.

Look at that sinless being,[2] agreeable (to look at) in every limb, with a chariot well made (down to) the spokes, (see her) clothed in a white gown,[3] and free yourself of the stream of bondage.[4]

28 (188).

The common of men, driven by fear, seek a refuge in mountains, forests, groves, sacrificial places, and in great trees.[5]

29 (189).

These are not the best of refuges, these are not the chief refuges, for a man who goes to them for a refuge is not freed from all suffering.

30 (190).

He who seeks a refuge in the Buddha, the law (dharma), and the church (sangha), (he who sees with understanding) suffering, the production of suffering, the destruction of suffering:

---

[1] The forest of desires.—P. The double signification of the Pâli *vana*, "forest" and "lust," is lost in the Tibetan translation.

[2] Spoken at the sight of the princess Kshema mounted on a chariot approaching to see Bhagavat.—P.

[3] Women travelling in waggons generally wear white gowns.—P.

[4] According to the Commentary, this verse is meant to imply: 1. "Agreeable in every limb" means morality; 2. "clothed in a white gown" means perfect freedom and perfect knowledge; 3. "pleasing spokes" means perfect memory, understanding, and meditation; 4. a chariot means correct views; it is consequently the way and its branches. The verse would consequently mean: "Look at that sinless being with correct views, morality, perfect memory, perfect understanding, &c., with perfect freedom, &c., do as she has done and destroy what holds you in bondage.

[5] Comp. Burnouf, *loc. cit.*, p. 187, and Apaṇṇaka Jâtaka.

SIGHT.

31 (191).

He who sees with understanding happiness, the way to nirvâṇa, the eightfold holy way and the four blessed truths:

32 (192).

This is the chief refuge, this is the holy refuge; he who goes to this refuge becomes freed from all suffering.[1]

33.

He who perceives (mentally) what he sees, can perceive also the unseen with his sight;[2] he who sees not the unseen does not perceive what he ought to see; ordinary sight[3] and spiritual insight (vipassanâ) are by their nature as different as day and night, which never are at the same time.

34.

With ordinary sight one cannot perceive (suffering, &c.); if one sees, he loses sight of form (rûpa);[4] with this sight (i.e., vipassanâ) one perceives not form; with ordinary sight one is without perceiving anything.[5]

35.

He who perceives nothing, sees (but) form; he who perceives, sees not form; thus they who perceive not form have freed themselves of ordinary sight (i.e., have obtained vipassanâ).[6]

---

[1] See Apaṇṇaka Jâtaka.

[2] He has *vipassanâ*, in Tibetan *lhag-mthong*, "sight which is free from any darkness (sin), which has overcome sin."—P.

[3] *Ildra-mthong*, "sight that has not been put to good account (*med-pa-la sgro-btags*)." *Ildra* means also "form, shape, body." The first two lines of this udâna, which is very obscure, are: *Mthong-bas mthong-dsing mthong-bas ma-mthong mthong ma-mthong mi mthong-bya mthong-mi hygur.*

[4] He loses sight of the self.—P.

[5] Not perceiving the state of the world, he does not perceive his own nature. The sight of the world is very coarse, and the truth (sight of truth?) very minute.—P.

[6] This verse is to sum up the teaching of the two preceding ones.

36.

When one perceives not suffering, then he considers but the self (*i.e.*, he has ordinary sight); but when one distinguishes suffering, then he perceives not form.

37.

He who is in the midst of darkness of repeated regeneration perceives not the suffering of the sanskâra, consequently he has but ordinary sight, and does not perceive how to put an end to form.

Chapter on Sight, the Twenty-seventh.

XXVIII.

SIN.

1 (183).

AVOID doing all wicked actions, practise most perfect virtue, thoroughly subdue your mind; this is the doctrine of the Buddha.[1]

2.

By charity one's merit is increased, by being well controlled one makes no enemies: the virtuous man, having cast off sin, puts an end to misery (kleça) and obtains nirvâṇa.[2]

3.

If the wise man is mixed with fools and lives in their midst, he remains separate; as one naturally drinks milk rather than water, so does the wise man cast away evil-doers.[3]

4.

Seeing all the wickedness of the world,[4] having seen the means to put an end to it, the elect take no pleasure in sin; the wicked cannot please the virtuous.

5.

He (the elect) knows the sweetness of perfect peace,

---

[1] See Pratimoxa Sûtra, 8; Mel. Asiat., viii. p. 591; Beal, Catena, p. 156; Vasubandhu's Gâthâsamgraha, 14; Mel. Asiat., viii. p. 564.

[2] Comp. Pratimoxa Sûtra, 7, loc. cit., p. 591.

[3] Who are like water.

[4] The sinfulness of transmigration, disease, old age, vice, &c.—P.

the sweetness of solitude; free from disease,[1] without sin, he drinks the sweetness of delighting in the law.

6.

His mind having done away with sins (âsrava), and not held by fetters, having cast off virtue and vice,[2] he (the elect) is without fear of the evil way.

7.

Having given up a house, speaking well, teaching what is sin, the wise man tells what puts an end to (life);[3] with such as he ought men to associate. If one associates with such as he, one is not made sinful but virtuous.

8.

He who is at rest and dispassionate, speaks with moderation and is without arrogance, he tears off all wickedness as does the wind the leaves of a tree.

9 (125).

The fool who is angered against a pure and sinless person who is without hatred, the sin falls back on him like dust thrown up against the wind.[4]

10.

By acts of virtue one is virtuous, by acts of wickedness one is wicked; a man will perceive himself (the consequence) of that which he has repeatedly done.[5]

---

[1] For ever free from pain.—P.

[2] "Virtue means here that, having cast off passions, and being without the material and the immaterial in the regions of perfect composure, one has cast off virtue" (??). "Vice means desires (trichnâ). Having cast off vice, there is no fear of evil births, and having cast off virtue, there is no fear of happy births."—P.

[3] *Tsar-gchod-smra-byed*, which, according to the Commentary, means "advising respect and earnest exertion."

[4] Comp. Sutra in 42 sections, viii. This verse was spoken on account of Varadhaja having sworn that Bhagavat had openly spoken wicked words to her, &c. According to another version, it was spoken of the deeds of the hunter Koka.—P.

[5] Spoken to illustrate the conduct of Ananda and of Dêvadatta, as are also the two next ones.

11 (165).

If by oneself evil has been done, oneself has all the suffering: if by oneself evil has been left undone, oneself is made pure: one cannot cleanse another; purity and impurity are one's own doings.

12 (161).

The sins that one has committed accumulate until they crush the fool, as a diamond pierces a precious stone.

13.

As the traveller who can see (avoids) the dangers, so does the wise man avoid the sins of the life in this world.[1]

14 (123).

As the merchant who has great treasures and few companions avoids dangerous roads, as he who loves life avoids poison, so let the sage avoid sinfulness.[2]

15 (124).

He who has no wound in his hand can take poison in his hand, for poison affects not him who has no wound; so likewise there is no evil for him who does not commit evil.[3]

16 (163).

Deeds that are hurtful to oneself and deeds that are wrong are easy to do; deeds that are beneficial and that bring happiness, they are very difficult to do.

17.

It is easy for the righteous to do right, it is difficult for the righteous to do evil; it is easy for the wicked to do evil, it is difficult for the elect (ariya) to do evil.

---

[1] Comp. Pratimoxa Sûtra, 2; Mel. Asiat., viii. p. 590.
[2] Comp. Beal, Dham., p. 154.
[3] Spoken of a man of Râjagriha called Kakuṭamitra, who having reached a great age had commenced giving up evil doings.—F.

18 (69).

As long as an evil deed has not ripened, the fool thinks that it is sweet; when an evil deed has ripened, then he perceives that it is burning.[1]

19 (119).

As long as an evil deed has not ripened, one thinks that it is right; when an evil deed has ripened, then one sees that it is evil.[2]

20 (120).

As long as a good deed has not ripened, good seems like evil; when a good deed has ripened, then one perceives it is good.

21 (117).

He who has laid up for himself the miseries of sin will find no joy; even if a man has done evil a hundred times, let him not do it again.

22 (118).

He who has laid up for himself the felicity of virtue will find joy; if a man had done what is virtuous, let him do it again.

23 (116).

The mind (of that man) delights in evil who does what is right slothfully; keeping his mind away from evil, he must hasten towards what is good.[3]

24.

He who has done even a little evil experiences in this world and in the other[4] great ruin and a great deal of

---

[1] Spoken in reply to a question of Anâthapindika. The three following verses were also spoken on the same occasion.

[2] Comp. Khadirangâra Jâtaka.

[3] Spoken on account of a Cûleka-sâtaka Brahman (*bram-ze ytsny-phud ras-gchiy*) in whom a spirit of charity had not arisen during ninety-nine kalpas.—P. Comp. Buddhaghosa's Commentary, Fausböll's Dhammapadam, p. 290.

[4] In this life and in the subsequent ones.—P.

suffering; it is like poison that has entered into the internal parts.¹

25.

He who has done even a little good finds in this world and in the other happiness and great profit; it is like a seed that has well taken root.

26 (137).

He who inflicts pain on one who is sinless, who is angered with one who is without anger, will speedily arrive himself at one of these ten states.²

27 (138).

He will experience no end of pain (vedana), or he will be torn limb from limb, or he will experience a heavy sensation of pain,³ or his mind will become deranged:

28 (139).

Or he will be separated from his relatives, or he will lose his wealth, or he will have some trouble with the king,⁴ or no end of disagreeable things:

29 (140).

Or yet, again, his home will be destroyed by a great fire;⁵ and when the senseless man has finished with this body he will go to hell.⁶

---

[1] M. Jäschke, s.v. "Khong," gives this last line as occurring in the Tibetan work entitled "Thar-gyan."

[2] This verse and the three following ones were spoken on account of the tortures inflicted on the Ariya Mâhamodgalyayana, who, having been tied like (a bundle) of reeds, had been crushed, &c., with the point of a stick. Others say it was on account of Shiṇkhandina (sic), who had killed his father, &c.—P. On the first version, see Spence Hardy, Manual, p. 349, and Fausböll, Dhammapadam, p. 298, et seq.

[3] *Gnod-pai tsor-ba lchi-ba.* This expression, which I think uncommon, is exactly copied in the Pâli, *garukam râpi âbâdham.*

[4] *Rgyal-poi gnod-pa hbyung ba-am,* lit. "there will be a trouble to the king;" but, besides the well-known use of the sign of the genitive for the dative (see Foucaux, Gram. Tib., p. 91), the Commentary says, "He will experience some great trouble from the ruler of the country; his good name will be lost, his abode will suffer, or he will be punished; it is as if he had insulted the king."—P.

[5] Fire from lightning.—P.

[6] Like Kokalita.—P. See chap. viii. verses 1-4.

30.

He who has done what is evil cannot free himself of it; he may have done it long ago or afar off,[1] he may have done it in solitude, but he cannot cast it off, and when it has ripened he cannot cast it off.[2]

31.

He who has done what is right is free of fear; he may have done it long ago or afar off, he may have done it in solitude; he is without fear, and when it (*i.e.*, his good deed) has ripened he is without fear.

32.

He who has done what is evil brings grief (on himself); though he has done it long ago or afar off, it brings sorrow; he may have done it in solitude, it brings sorrow; and when it has ripened it brings him sorrow.

33 (15).

When one has seen one's evil deeds, one has sorrow here and one will have sorrow in the other world; the evil-doer has sorrow in both places; he mourns and will greatly sorrow.

34.

He who has done what is right is made happy; (though) he has done it long ago and afar off, he is made happy; he may have done it in solitude, (but) he is made happy; and when it has ripened it brings him joy.[3]

---

[1] The fruit of an evil deed is like seed which, though one has forgotten when it was put in the ground, is not destroyed.—P.

[2] This verse and the next one were spoken by Bhagavat on being told that "there were two sons of a merchant of Çravasti, young men of a same age (*neu-ldangs?*); one had conceived an infinite faith in the Triratna, while the other was without faith and avaricious. It came to pass that they both died, and the former was born in the Tushita heaven while the latter went to hell.—P.

[3] Spoken on account of the virtuous life of the Ariyâ Somanâsa, who had been reborn in the world of the gods.—P.

35 (16).

When one has seen one's righteous deeds, one rejoices here and will also rejoice in the other (world); he who has done what is right rejoices in both places; he is made glad, he will be exceedingly joyful.

36.

He who has done what is evil is made to suffer; though he has done it long ago, though he has done it afar off, he is made to suffer; though he has done it in solitude, he is made to suffer; and when it has ripened it brings him suffering.

37 (17).

When one has seen one's evil deeds,[1] one suffers in this (world); one will suffer in the next (world); the evil-doer suffers in both; he suffers and he will greatly suffer.

38.

He who has done what is right is made happy; (though) he has done it long ago, (though) he has done it afar off, he is made happy; though he has done it in solitude he is made happy; and when it has ripened he is made happy.[2]

39 (18).

When one has seen one's righteous deeds [3] one rejoices here and will rejoice in the other world; he who has done what is right rejoices in both places; he is made glad, he will be made exceedingly joyful.

40.

He who has done evil and has not done what was right,

---

[1] *Naʒ-poi las*, "black deeds."

[2] The only point in which this verse differs from No. 34 is in the second line; it is, however, a mere repetition. The Commentary does not mention this verse.

[3] *Dkar-poi las*, "white deeds." In verse 35 there is *rnam-dag*, "perfectly pure;" this and the use here of *pha-rol* instead of *gdsan-du*, "other world," constitute the sole difference between these two verses.

who strays away from the law, who is an unbeliever, the wicked man is in fear of death, like one on a great river in a leaky (lit. bad) boat.[1]

41.

He who has been virtuous and has done what is right, who follows the doctrines of the holy men of old,[2] he has never any fear of death, like one in a strong boat which can reach the other shore.[3]

Chapter on Sin, the Twenty-eighth.

---

[1] When the Bodhisattva was seated on the diamond throne (vadjrasana), thirty-six koti of demons had assailed him with all kinds of weapons and instruments. Then afterwards the devas swiftly went to the Bodhi-tree, and surrounding the Bodhisattva, they joined their hands and asked him, "Hadst thou no fear of Mára and all his great hosts?" Then the Bodhisattva repeated these two verses of a former Táthagata.—P. See Lalita Vistara (Foucaux's translation), p. 320.

[2] The perfect Buddha Kaçyapa, &c.—P.

[3] Compare Návásutta (Sutta Nipáta), 6.

XXIX.

DAY AND NIGHT.[1]

1.

As long as the sun has not risen the glow-worm doth shine; when the sun has risen he is without brightness, and becomes as he formerly was.[2]

2.

As long as the Tathâgata had not appeared the sophists[3] did shine; when the perfectly Enlightened One appeared in the world, teachers and disciples shined no more.

3 (11).

He who considers that which is not precious as precious,[4] and who thinks that what is precious is not precious, his whole understanding entirely subverted, he will not find what is precious.

---

[1] *Phrugs.* According to M. Jäschke, p. 354, "one day with the night, a period of twenty-four hours; but this signification does not hold good in every case." It is evidently used here to express "both day and night," the two forming a pair (*yamaka*). M. Beal informs me that the title of this chapter in the Chinese version is "Yamaka."

[2] Comp. Burnouf, Introd., p. 185, where this verse and the following one are found in the Prâtihârya Sûtra, and are addressed by Bhagavat to his philosophical opponents. The Commentary attributes the same origin to them.

[3] *Rtog-ge* = Sansk. *tarka*, "logician."

[4] What is precious are the facts (*gtam*) sight, meditation, freedom. The facts comprise the impermanency of created things, the suffering of all the âsravas, the freedom of nirvâṇa, &c.

4 (12).

He who perceives that what is not precious is not precious, and that what is precious is precious, his whole understanding properly arranged, he will find what is precious.

5.

They who are again and again adding to their bonds through their fondness for these (theories), and giving ear to them, flitting about in the orb of transmigration, they like the moths fall into the fire.[1]

6.

When one in this world has any kind of uncertainty about the enjoyment here (of the maturity of one's actions) or the enjoyment hereafter, if he is living a life of holiness (brahmachariya), when he has thought on it, (his doubts) will be entirely removed.

7 (9).

He whose (mind) is like troubled water, and who wears the saffron-coloured gown, being without restraint, he is not worthy of the saffron-coloured gown.[2]

8 (10).

He who has cast off all impurities, whose mind is attentive to the moral laws, being thus restrained, he is worthy of the saffron-coloured gown.[3]

9.

The artful, deceitful, and avaricious man, notwith-

---

[1] (Bhagavat being at) Çrâvasti at the time of the Kumuda feast in the fourth month, had gone from Djêtavana into Çrâvasti at night, when it was lit up with lamps. And there having observed the moths falling into the burning offerings (*thab-bshos*) of the crowd of coming and going Tirthikas, he exclaimed, "They fall, they fall!" and then he added the words of the text.—P.

[2] Spoken at Veluvana on account of the evil doings of Kokalita.

[3] Like the colour of the root of a tree.—P.

standing the colour (of his gown), his appearance, and what he may say, has not become the best of men.

10.

He who has cut down these three characteristics (of the sinner)[1] as he would the top of a tâla-tree, intelligent and cleansed of sins, he is called the best of men.

11.

He who in this world, not being well controlled, deceitfully, for some interested motive, produces the incorrect idea that he is well controlled by the general appearance of his garb (lit. colour and person), no confidence must be placed in him.

12.

As deceiving as the colour of brass, like iron coated over with gold is he whose inside is poison, and whose outward manner is that of the elect, and who goes about in this world with a great company.[2]

13 (325).

He who is given to gourmandising, to sleeping, to going about day and night seeking for a place to lie down in, like a great hog (wallowing) in the mire, this man will be reborn again and again.

---

[1] Tchos = dharma; they are imposture, cunning, and avarice, alluded to in the preceding verse.

[2] At a certain time seven naked ascetics, seven ascetics with hair mats (skrai la-ba chan), and seven ascetics with one garment, with well-conditioned bodies, were living together at the gates of Djêtavâna. King Prasênajit, having remarked them, rose from his seat, threw his mantle over one shoulder, and with joined hands he listened three times to their words. After a while Bhagavat asked him, "Why did you do thus?" "Venerable one," he answered, "I thought they were Arhats in this world." "Great king, you are wrong; but as you cannot distinguish an Arhat and one who is not one, of course you cannot know (the difference) in their ideas. Great king, all those that are here together, though they have the bearing (of Arhats), will not, even after a great space of time, have the knowledge. Not even comprehending this, what knowledge can they possess? How can they know steadfastness in time of need, what is a life of purity, (true) words and coherent words?" Then he spoke these two verses (11-12).—P.

14.

The man who is always thoughtful, who knows how to be always moderate in his food, he is subject to but little suffering,[1] and his slow digestion prolongs his life.[2]

15 (7).

He whose senses are not controlled, who does not know how to be moderate in his food, who is thoughtless and idle, who lives seeking what pleases (the eye),[3] is overthrown by his passions as is a weak tree by the wind.

16 (8).

He whose senses are well controlled, who knows how to be moderate in his food, who remembers everything[4] and is diligent, who seeks not after what pleases (the eye), is not disturbed by passions, like a mountain unshaken by the wind.

17 (99).

The forest is delightful, where man finds no delight; there the passionless finds delight, for he seeks not after pleasures.

18 (98).

In a forest or in a village, on a mountain top or in a valley,[5] in whatever part of the earth an Ariya dwells, that (spot) is agreeable.

---

[1] He is not made ill by flatulency, &c.—P.

[2] "Prince Prasênajit was so very fat, that though at rest, he was covered with perspiration. Having had the energy to go to where Bhagavat was, he said, 'Venerable one, my person is so stout and cumbersome, and annoys me so much, that it causes me to blush.'"—P. See Beal, *loc. cit.*, p. 134.

[3] *Gtsang-mar lta dsing*, "one does what is pleasing in looking at the persons of women."—P. *Gtsang-ma*, "what is neat, tidy." It is used here for the Pâli *subha*, "pleasure, radiant, lustrous."

[4] *So-sor dran-dsing*, i.e., "remembering what appertains to the body."—P. That it is impermanent, &c. (?)

[5] *Bshong dam thang-du.* Compare the Pâli, *ninne va yadiva thale*, which, according to Childers, might be translated, "on low ground or on high ground." But it has always been translated by "in mari vel in terra."

19 (304).

The holy shine from afar off, like the snowy mountains; the wicked shine not, even though near, like arrows shot in intense darkness.

20.

If one associates with the wise, with the holy whose minds are turned to virtue, he obtains great profit,[1] and acquires profound wisdom.

21 (320).

As the elephant in battle (is patient though) pierced by the arrows shot from the bows, so likewise be patient under the unkind words of the crowd.[2]

22.

He who makes a cave his abode,[3] who has nothing to do with the unrighteous, who suppresses all contingencies,[4] and who lives on refuse (?),[5] that man is holy.

23.

Having killed father and mother and two holy kings, having conquered their kingdoms with its inhabitants a man will be pure.[6]

24 (92).

He who is without concupiscence, who is always moderate in his food, the field of whose activity is the void,

---

[1] The truth concerning suffering, &c.—P.

[2] According to the text of the Bstan-hgyur and also the Commentary, the following verse ought to be placed between 21 and 22:—"The common of mortals are in the orb of decay, but I have found out its awfulness, therefore there is no pleasure (for me) in existence, and having found out what accompanies existence, I delight not in it."

[3] *Khyim hbigs byed pa*, my translation is uncertain.

[4] *Go-skabs bchan*. "There being no causes, there can be no effects."—P. According to M. Jäschke, *go-skabs* means "a chance of taking place, a possibility."

[5] *Skyugs-pa za*. "He is without fondness, having finished with existence."—P. I translate *skyugs-pa* conjecturally.

[6] See Appendix. Comp. xxxiii. v. 70, and Dham. 294. Or it may be translated, "a king and two pure men."

K

the uncharacteristic, and solitude, his way [1] is difficult to perceive, like that of birds in the ether.[2]

25 (93).

He who is without concupiscence, who is always moderate in his food, the field of whose activity is the void, the uncharacteristic, and solitude, his track [3] is difficult to perceive like the track of birds in the ether.

26.

He who is without concupiscence, who is always moderate in his food, the field of whose activity is the void, the uncharacteristic, and continual contemplation (dhyâna), his way is difficult to perceive, like the track of birds in the ether.

27.

He who is without concupiscence, who is always moderate in his food, the field of whose activity is the void, the uncharacteristic, and continual contemplation, his track is difficult to perceive, like the track of birds in the ether.

28, 29.

(Repetitions of verses 24 and 25.)

30.

He who is not held to this shore, who has found out the cessation of the âsravas, the field of whose activity is the void, the uncharacteristic, and solitude, his way is difficult to perceive, like the track of birds in the ether.

31.

He who is not held to this shore, who has found out the cessation of the âsravas, the field of whose activity is

---

[1] *Hgro-ba = gati.*
[2] Comp. Book of Wisdom, v. 11.
[3] *Rjes-pa = pada.*

the void, the uncharacteristic, and solitude, his track is difficult to perceive, like the track of birds in the ether.

32.

He who is not held to this shore, who has found out the cessation of the âsravas, the field of whose activity is the void, the uncharacteristic, and continual contemplation, his way is difficult to perceive, like the track of birds in the ether.

33.

He who is not held to this shore,[1] who has found out the cessation of the âsravas, the field of whose activity is the void, the uncharacteristic, and continual meditation, his track is difficult to perceive, like the track of birds in the ether.

34, 35.

(Repetitions of verses 32 and 33.)

36 (85).

The common of mortals run along this shore; few there are among men who go to the other shore.[2]

37 (86).

Those beings who walk in the way of the law that has been well taught, reach the other shore of the great sea of birth and death, that is difficult to cross.

38.

He who frees himself by watchfulness,[3] who leaves in the past all sorrows, one who thus delivers himself of all his bonds, will know no affliction whatever.

39.

When one passes beyond the road of terror and what

---

[1] Not being subject to future births, having cast off passions.—P.
[2] Who arrive at nirvâṇa.—P.
[3] By separation from all carnal passions.—P.

accompanies it,[1] and is out of the way of precipices (*i.e.*, falling into the evil way), freed of all bonds and ties, he has destroyed the poison of the passions.

40 (251).

There is no swamp like desire (trichnâ); there is nothing as pernicious as hatred; there is no net like ignorance; there is no torrent like covetousness.

41.

The Çramana who has reached the other shore is like the trackless firmament;[2] the fool delights in his occupations, and the Tathâgata is not his occupation. The fool is led through (attachment); the wise man destroys all attachment.

42.

The wise man destroys all attachments of gods and men, and by being free from all attachment he becomes emancipated from all suffering.

43.

From attachment[3] proceeds existence; without attachment there is no existence: to the acquisition of the knowledge of these two ways of existence and not existence and the way to be perfectly delivered of attachment, let the wise man apply himself.

44.

He who has done that which is wrong, suffers for it, and when hereafter he will be in the evil way he will suffer; he who has done that which is right, is made happy, and when hereafter he will be in the happy way he will be happy.[4]

---

[1] He who leaves behind all evil ways. P.
[2] Lit. like a path in the firmament. —P.
[3] Attachment (*shyor*) to existence, to desires, to (false) theories, to ignorance. The kleças of the three regions. —P.
[4] *Cf.* verses 42, 43, with xxviii. 37, 38.

45.

It is better in both (this world and the other) if one has not done evil, for he who does it will suffer; it is good for one to do what is right, for he will have no affliction.

46.

The wise man and the fool being mixed together, it is not possible to distinguish them when they have not spoken; but let one of them impart (the way) to the perfection of peace (nirvâṇa), then he is known by his speech (to be a sage).

47.

The expounding (of the law) is the standard of the Rischi (*i.e.*, Bhagavat); the law being the standard of the Rischi, and the law by his explanations being made brilliant, let the Rischi raise on high his standard.

48 (227).

If one has not spoken he is blamed; if one has spoken much he is blamed; he who speaks slowly is blamed: there is no one in the world who is not blamed.

49 (228).

A man who is only to be blamed, or one who is only to be praised, there is none such; there never has been, there never will be.

50.

They who preoccupy not themselves about existence, who have put an end to all return of suffering from attachment, and are delivered of existence, gods and men cannot understand their purpose.[1]

51 (229, 230).

He who is praised by those who have discriminative knowledge, as being faithful, virtuous, and of great wis-

---

[1] *Rgyu-mtsad.* This verse in the Commentary is placed after verse 53; it may be Dhammapada, 181.

dom,[1] there is no one who can blame him; he is like a jewel of Djambudvipa gold.

52 (81).

As mountains and rocks are unshaken by the wind, so likewise the wise man is unmoved by praise or blame.[2]

53.

The earnest man without any root in the earth, without a leaf (of sinfulness) on any branch, delivered from bondage, there is no one who can blame him.

54 (179).

He who does not suffer from conquest, whom the world cannot conquer in the least, the Buddha, the field of whose activity is infinite, there is no being by whose steps he is guided.[3]

55.

He who does not suffer from conquest, whom the world cannot conquer in the least, the Buddha, whose might is infinite, there is no being by whose steps he is guided.

56 (180).

He to whom the allurements of desires and the regions of desire have no delight, the Buddha, the field of whose activity is infinite, there is no being by whose steps he is guided.

57.

He to whom the allurements of desires and the region of desire have no delight, the Buddha, whose might is infinite, there is no being by whose steps he is guided.

---

[1] *Blo-la hphan ni ma-byung-bar.* I am unable to translate this literally; the Commentary explains it by saying, "doing continually what is virtuous, having wisdom."

[2] *Cf.* Jatakanidânam, Mdo xxx. f. 458a, and Fausböll's Jataka, p. 24, gâtha 163. The udâna is evidently an adaptation of the gâtha of the Jataka.

[3] King Çuddhôdana becoming desirous of seeing (again) Bhagavat's face, sent a messenger towards him, with instructions that if he would not come of himself he must bring him by force. Bhagavat spoke the four following verses (54-57).—P.

58.

He who is illumined by perfect understanding, who having fathomed everything abides in nothing, who is delivered of all attachments, of form, and consciousness (saudjâ), who has got rid of the four yogas,[1] he has put an end to birth.

59 (348).

Having cast off what is before, having cast off what is behind, having cast off what is in the middle, one goes to the other shore of existence; when the mind is free from everything, one will not be subject to birth and death.

Chapter of "Day and Night," the Twenty-ninth.

---

[1] According to the Commentary, these are the four Ayatanas alluded to in chap. xxvi. 26. This is only true as far as the four Ayatanas correspond with the four Samapatti of the invisible world. The text implies that he has given up all fondness for the invisible world.

XXX.

HAPPINESS.

1 (201).

From victory proceeds rancour; the defeated foe is in misery: if one casts off victory and defeat he will find the happiness of peace.

2 (291).

He who causes misery to others in seeking for his own welfare brings without distinction misery on friends and foes.

3 (131).

He who seeking happiness persecutes and punishes other beings also seeking for happiness, will not find happiness in the other world.

4 (132).

He who seeking happiness does not persecute and punish beings seeking for happiness, will find happiness in the other world.

5 (169).

Perform carefully the precepts of the law; abstain from all evil deeds: he who keeps the law finds happiness in this world and in the other.

6.

The observance of the law brings happiness; he who keeps the law is guarded by the law; he who keeps the law goes not on the evil way; for this is the observance of the law beneficial.

7.

He who keeps the law is sheltered by the law, as is one in summer by a large umbrella; he who keeps the law goes not on the evil way, for this reason is the observance of the law beneficial.

8.

The careless man who observes not the law, no matter who he may be, goes to damnation; he who keeps not the law is as surely destroyed as is the black snake that one has caught by the middle.

9.

The rewards of the righteous and of the unrighteous are not the same; the unrighteous go to hell, the righteous find the way to happiness.

10, 11.

When one is charitable and when one gives battle, if well understood these (operations) are primarily alike;[1] as I have said (or it has been said) that being charitable and fighting are alike, be careful in both cases and rely not on what is bad. A single man well equipped can conquer (a legion) of badly equipped rabble (?),[2] so likewise if one gives through faith, even though a little, he will thereby find happiness in the other world.

12.

He who has been victorious in a hundred battles, and who has overcome all his enemies, is not so great a conqueror, I declare, as he who gives with a pure heart.

---

[1] They are both the means of acquiring fame and great profit.

[2] *Legs-par mat chas hphyes-las rgyal.* The Commentary explains it by "he will conquer innumerable enemies." *Hphyes*, according to the dictionaries, means "to creep, to crawl like a snake."

13.

The reward of virtue is happiness; he who has made this his goal will speedily find perfect rest and nirvâṇa.[1]

14.

There is nothing by which men can harm them who are virtuous; they from the world of the gods and of Mâra are not able to hurt them.

15.

He who, to put an end to misery, applies himself diligently to the acquirement of righteousness and knowledge, shall enjoy (it) through supernatural sight (vipaçyana).

16.

He who delights in the law[2] with a truly believing mind, finds happiness; the sage always delights in the law that has been taught by the elect.

17, 18.

They whose minds delight in contemplation (dhyana),[3] who delight in no created thing, who delight in the four modes of arranging the memory,[4] in the seven branches of the Bodhi, in the four bases of performing miracles,[5] in the eightfold way, they wear the garment of the law and are happy in living on alms.

19.

They move about in peace on mountains and in forests; they are happy in finding happiness, and leave sorrow behind in the perception of the law (nirvâṇa). He has

---

[1] This verse occurs with a slight variation in Vasubandhu's Gâthâ-samgraha, No. 17. See Mel. Asiat., viii. pp. 564, 568, and Appendix.
[2] "Law means the truth concerning suffering."—P.
[3] The Commentary considers this as synonymous of *samâdhi* and *sgom-pa* (meditation).
[4] Tchatuh smrityupasthâna. See Burnouf, Intr., p. 626 *et seq.*
[5] *Riddhipâda*; see Trig., fol. 17; Burnouf, *loc. cit.*, p. 625, and Childers, s.v. "Iddhipâdo."

left behind hatred and fear, and has crossed over from worldly existence.

20.

To hear the law, to perceive the law, and to delight in seclusion, is happiness; to all living beings in the world to comprehend the complete cessation of death is happiness.

21.

To abandon desires, to be free of the passions of the world, is happiness; to subdue the selfish thought of "I" is the greatest happiness.

22 (333).

To be virtuous unto old age is happiness; to live in perfect faith is happiness; to delight in words of sense is happiness; to do no evil is happiness.

23 (332).

Happy in this world is he who honours his father,[1] so likewise he who honours his mother is happy; happy in this world he who honours Çramanas, so likewise he who honours Brâhmanas is happy.

24 (194).

The arising of a Buddha is happiness, the teaching of the law is happiness, the harmony of the clergy is happiness, the devotion (tapas) of those who are united is happiness.

25.

'Tis happiness to see a virtuous man; to see one who has heard much is happiness; to see Arhats who are delivered from existence is happiness.

---

[1] *Phar hdsin pa*, "to agree completely with one's father is a source of great merit, and much to be praised." — P. *Cf.* Max Müller's translation.

26.

'Tis happiness to reach the shore of the river of happiness; happy the being who has the triumph of the law (*i.e.*, who has attained purity); to obtain wisdom is happiness; to put an end to selfishness is happiness.

27 (206).

To see the elect is happiness; to associate with the righteous is happiness; not to see fools is always happiness.[1]

28 (207).

'Tis as great suffering to be in the company of fools as in that of enemies; he who associates with fools will repent him of it for a long time.

29 (193).

An omniscient person[2] is hard to find; he does not appear everywhere: 'tis happiness to associate with the steadfast, like unto meeting one's kinsmen; wherever such a steadfast person is born, that people finds happiness.

30.

The Brâhmanas who have left sorrow behind, find most perfect happiness; he who has divested himself of desires, who is without âsravas, is perfectly free.

31.

They who have destroyed all desires, who have cleansed their hearts of all cankers,[3] their minds bring them peace, and in peace there is happiness.

32 (290).

If the steadfast man seeks for great happiness, and

---

[1] Verses 21-27 are taken from the Introduction of the Pratimoxa. See Dulva, ix. f. 3a.

[2] Çariputra was receiving great marks of respect, the crowds were decorating the roads, &c.—P.

[3] Such as anger, hatred, &c.—P.

would give up little happiness, let him cast away the little happiness and look well to the great one.[1]

33.

Worldly happiness and happiness in the region of the gods is not worth the sixteenth part of the happiness (resulting) from the destruction of desires.

34.

If one has been miserable under the weight of his burden,[2] 'tis happiness to cast it down; if one has cast down his heavy load, he will not in future take up another.

35.

He who has put an end to all attachment, who has cast away all affection, who perfectly understands all the skandhas, will not be subject to any subsequent existence.

36.

To associate with those who bring one great profit is happiness; to be virtuous in the different circumstances of life is happiness; to be satisfied with no matter how mean a pittance is happiness; to put an end to all suffering is happiness.

37.

By beating with a hammer the iron that has been burnt with fire it is finally destroyed; in like manner is the unwise man done away with.

---

[1] In the country of Verashâna (Viraçâna? See Stan. Julien, Si-yu-ki, Book iv. p. 235), a sthavira called Sinha had died. His disciple (sekhas) said to the Bhixus who had come thither, "Honour my master (upâdhyâya) who has passed away, for he (has gone to) great wealth." Bhagavat hearing that (Sinha) had left behind every remnant of the skandhas, &c., went that way, and having heard the request (of the disciple), he said, "Your upâdhyâya is enjoying to its full extent the happiness of the land of the three dhyanas, where he has been born."—P.

[2] The skandhas. There may have been in the original some pun on the word *skandha* (*phung-po*), "heap, accumulation." This verse and the following one were spoken on the same occasion to teach the Bhixus what "burden" meant.—P.

38.

He who, having forded the miry stream of desire, has found the unchanging place (amatam padam, nirvâṇa), there is nothing that will hold back that being who has (found) perfect emancipation.

39.

He whom nothing agitates, who has left existence and not existence, free of terror, happy and without sorrow, even the gods on seeing (his happiness) cannot comprehend its (extent).

40.

In this world to hear much of the law and to comprehend it, nothing is so great a happiness! Man is filled with love for his body, and see how little it takes to destroy it![1]

42.

He who has understood that there is nothing commendable in the human condition, will have the happiness of never being subject to birth; man is filled with love for his body, and see how little it takes to destroy it!

43.

While it is misery to be in subjection to another, to be one's own master is great happiness; 'tis hard to cast off attachment, and to put an end to the source of all troubles.

---

[1] This verse and the next one were spoken on the following occasion. King Prasenajit had ordered for a limited time (*gtan-pa med-pa*) a distribution of melted butter and sesame oil (tila); no one was to carry any home, but he was allowed for a short space of time to partake of as much as he liked. A parivradjaka, his wife having brought forth a child, required some grease; so he went to the hall, and after having drunk a great quantity of melted butter, he started for his home. "My wife will be well satisfied," he thought; but the quantity of butter he had drunk could not be digested, and he fell (dead?) in the street. Ananda told the event to Bhagavat, &c.—P. Ver. 41 is omitted as being a repetition of ver. 40.

HAPPINESS.

44 (199).

Ah! let us live exceedingly happy, living without greed among men who are greedy, without greed in the midst of the greedy.

45 (198).

Ah! let us live exceedingly happy, living without disease among men afflicted by diseases, without disease in midst of disease.

46.

Ah! let us live exceedingly happy, living without enmity amidst men who are inimical, without enmity among the inimical.

47.

Ah! let us live exceedingly happy, living without cruel thoughts amidst men who have cruel thoughts, without cruelty among the cruel.

48.

Ah! let us live exceedingly happy, living without hatred amidst men who hate, without hatred among haters.

49.

Ah! let us live exceedingly happy; though Mithilâ burns, nothing of mine does burn, for I have nothing.[1]

50 (200).

Ah! let us live exceedingly happy; though there be nothing to call our own, we shall feed on happiness like the shining gods.[2]

---

[1] See Mahâbharata, xii. 9917, and Max Müller's Dhammapada, p. 53, note. "There once lived a king of Mithilâ who had become a Rischi, and had cast off desires and passions. Having perceived Mithilâ in flames, he spoke a gâtha that had been spoken by a (former) Buddha. — P.

[2] $Od\text{-}gsal = âbhâsvara$. See Burnouf, Intr., p. 611; Rgya-tcher rolpa, p. 143, 340, &c.; and Brahmajâla Sûtra, Mdo xxx. f. 115a, where their existence is described.

51.

Ah! let us live exceedingly happy, relying on nothing perishable; and though there be nothing to call our own, we shall feed on happiness.

52.

When one meets with the consequences of attachment (upadana) one must suffer; when there is no attachment there is nothing to meet which can cause suffering; he who has finished with both the one and the other (attachment and its consequences) and is happy, will not have to endure affliction in either forest or hamlet.[1]

53.

In this world the holy man is neither elated or depressed by joy or sorrow; the steadfast are not made vain by the objects of desire;[2] the holy man forsakes everything.

Chapter on Happiness, the Thirtieth.

---

[1] This verse is rather difficult. I have followed the suggestions of the Commentary, but have been obliged to translate rather freely.
[2] Profit and honours.— P.

BOOK IV.

Book IV.

XXXI.

THE MIND.

1 (35).

It is good to control the mind, which is difficult to hold, unstable, and which goes where it pleases: with a controlled mind one acquires happiness.

2 (34).

To escape from the abode of Mâra one is filled with trembling, like a fish taken from its watery abode and thrown on dry land.

3.

Like one deprived of the light of the sun, one's mind wanders about; they who are truly wise hold it in, as one does an elephant with an iron hook.

4.

It is not "do that which is of no profit to oneself, which is not worth a thought, which is of no import; but continually to control your mind" — that is what I say.

5 (326).

Formerly this mind (of mine) ran about as it wanted,

as suited its fancy; now it is orderly, and I hold it in as does the man with a hook¹ a maddened elephant.

6 (153).

Maker of the house, I have sought until now to find thee,² going through the revolution of countless existences, and subject to the pain of ever-recurring birth.

7 (154).

Maker of the house, having found thee out, and the great beams of the house (kleça) being destroyed, and all the rafters (trichnâ)³ hewn down, thou shalt not hereafter make a house (for me).⁴

8 (33).

When one, having freed the mind of the sanskâra, would put an end to it (birth), the mind being uncertain, changeable, flighty, and hard to control, he must straighten it by application as the fletcher straightens (his arrows) with fire.

9.

He who, thinking not of the body, lives in a cave, and wanders about all alone, does conquer this flighty mind, and is delivered of the greatest of terrors.

---

[1] *Mi-yis lchags-kyus* = a mahout, in Pâli *ankusaggaho*.

[2] *Khyod-khyis phyung*, "I have gone again and again to find thee really out, source of existence." *Phyung* is part. pret. of *hbyin-pa*, "to draw forth, to bring to light." The third line, *skye-bai hkhor ba-du-ma dsig*, seems to be a translation of the Pâli *samsarati* = sandhâvati (sandhâvissam), in which case *dsig* might be the aorist of *hjig-pa*. The Commentary, however, does not explain this line as if it represented a compound.

[3] Or affection instead of kleça, and ignorance instead of trichnâ, according to other opinions.—P.

[4] A person who had entered the priesthood after giving up a householder's life was admonished by Bhagavat (in these verses) when being disconsolate. According to another account, they were spoken by the Bodhisattva while dwelling near the Bo tree, when the envoys, &c., of Mâra came to trouble his mind.—P. Comp. Beal, Romantic Legend, p. 45. Also the version of the Jatakanidânam in the Introduction. See also Rgya tcher rol-pa (Lalita Vistara), p. 365 of the Tibetan text. "I have had created in me the perception of knowledge; I have finished with birth," &c.

10 (42).

He whose mind is evilly inclined will bring suffering on himself, as will not a hater by hatred, as will not an enemy to an enemy.

11 (43).

He whose mind is virtuously inclined will bring happiness on himself, as cannot bring father, mother, and the other relatives.

12 (13).

As into the badly-covered house pours the rain, so likewise is the unmeditative mind overwhelmed by lust.

13.

As into the badly-covered house pours the rain, so likewise is the unmeditative mind overwhelmed by passions.

14 (14).

As into the well-covered house drops not the rain, so the meditative mind keeps out the rising passions.

15.

As into the badly-covered house pours the rain, so is the unmeditative mind overwhelmed by ignorance (tamas).

16.

As into the well-covered house drops not the rain, so the meditative mind keeps out rising ignorance.

17.

As into the badly-covered house pours the rain, so is the unmeditative mind overwhelmed by selfishness.

18.

As into the well-covered house drops not the rain, so the meditative mind keeps out rising selfishness.

19.

As into the badly-covered house pours the rain, so is the unmeditative mind overwhelmed by affections.[1]

20.

As into the well-covered house drops not the rain, so the meditative mind keeps out rising affections.

21.

As into the badly-covered house pours the rain, so is the unmeditative mind overwhelmed by desires.

22.

As into the well-covered house drops not the rain, so the meditative mind keeps out rising desires.

23 (1).

The mind is the leader of its faculties (dharma); the mind is swift; the mind is the ruler: if one has either spoken or acted with evil intent, he will experience suffering, as he whose head was cut off by a wheel.[2]

24 (2).

The mind is the leader of its faculties;[3] the mind is swift; the mind is the ruler: if one has either spoken or acted with pure intent, he will find happiness (as surely) as one's shadow follows one's track.

---

[1] *Tchags* = attachments. Throughout these verses (12-22) the Tibetan uses the plural "ignorances, selfishnesses," &c.

[2] The origin of this verse and the next is briefly this: Two merchants had heard the Buddha preach recommending that when one had eaten enough he should give to another what was left. One of the merchants spoke offensively of the Buddha and his disciples, the other one in terms of great praise. A short time after, while lying under a tree sleeping, the wheel of a waggon passed over the former and killed him. See Beal, Dhamm., pp. 62, 63.

[3] Of ideas, of virtue, and wickedness.—P.

25.

He who is greatly given to wrangling, whose mind is sinful, though he may seek the means to do so, cannot well understand what has been well explained.[1]

26.

They who are angered or quarrelsome, or whose minds are without faith, cannot understand the blessed law taught by the perfect Buddha.

27.

They who, their minds without impurity and with anger perfectly subdued, have cast off all evil-mindedness, they by this means can understand what is well explained.

28.

He whose mind is not steadfast cannot understand the holy law; he whose faith is fickle cannot acquire perfect wisdom.

29 (339).

He who, given up to the indulgence of pleasure, is held in the stream of the thirty-six evil ideas, will be swept away by the flood of his passions.

30.

Thoughts of pleasure and subjection to the senses pursue the mind, demolishing the weak man's bright lot,[2] like birds do the fruits on a tree.

---

[1] At Çravasti, a Brahman called Pipralikasâri, proficient in all the false theories of the Brahmans, went to where Bhagavat was, and said: "Bho Gautama (*kye gautama*), tell me the dharma, and I will listen to it," &c. According to another version, Tchandasri, minister of Adjatasatru, a man who delighted in killing and cruelty, to promote the interests of Devadatta, had offered to give three hundred villages to him who would kill Çakyamuni, &c. See Spence Hardy, Manual, p. 330. Verses 25-27 were spoken on this occasion.

[2] *Grags*, lit. "glory, renown"—*grags-pa ni sñan pao*—or, according to other authorities, "the excellency to which he may have attained." The first line is obscure—*sems dyah dbang-po*(?) *phal-pa dang*. The Bk. reads *dad-po* or *dang-po*. The Comment., *dbang-po*.

31 (371).

Delight not thy mind in seeking what is dazzling; keep thy mind diligent and pure, that thou mayest not for thy wicked deeds, being born in hell, have to weep on swallowing the iron ball.

32 (280).

He who remains seated when it is time to rise, who, though strong and young, sits slothfully at home, who is always careless in his thoughts, will not find the road to wisdom.

33.

They who, though understanding what is trifling (*i.e.*, desires), and understanding (the importance of) passionlessness, have their innermost mind still disturbed,[1] have not thorough understanding; their minds are deceived, and they wander about (in the orb of transmigration) again and again.

34.

They whose memory is perfectly developed, who are diligent, who discriminate, the wise, they have understanding, and by means of their intellect they cast away every one of the errors in the interior of the mind.

35 (40).

He who has discerned that this body is like a vase, having by his thoughts made this (idea) as lasting as a citadel, fights Mâra with wisdom as a weapon; and having overcome him, he will keep to a houseless state.[2]

36.

He who has discerned that this world is like a vase (*i.e.*, empty), having by his thoughts made this (idea) as lasting as a citadel, fights Mâra with wisdom as a weapon;

---

[1] Whose mind consequently is not controlled. In Pâli *anivasano siya*. See Max Muller's Dhamm., p. 14.

[2] *Gnas-med par ni bsrung-bar bya.*

THE MIND.

and having overcome him, he will keep to a houseless state.

37.

He who has discerned that this body is like froth, having by his thoughts made this (idea) as lasting as a citadel, fights Mâra with wisdom as a weapon; and having overcome him, he will keep to a houseless state.

38.

He who has discerned that this world is like froth, having by his thoughts made this (idea) as lasting[1] as a citadel, fights Mâra with wisdom as a weapon; and having overcome him, he will keep to a houseless state.

39 (89).

He whose mind is devoted to meditating on the seven branches of the bodhi, who is free from all attachment (upadana), who has cast off attachment, is cleansed of the stains of misery, and goes beyond sorrow (parinibbuta) in this world.[2]

40.

He who watches over his mind as does the yak over the end of its tail, is merciful to all creatures, and his happiness will not grow less (in this world).[3]

41.

He whose mind is well composed (not given to anger), delights in living alone (like) the largest of elephants, the elephant with goodly tusks.[4]

42.

He whose mind knows no harm, who is kind to all

---

[1] *Sran - btsugs*, "enduring, hard, &c." According to the Comment., "thoroughly understanding this idea, &c."

[2] This gâtha was spoken on hearing of the death of the ayuchmat, Çâriputra. Comp. chap. xxxii. 32.

[3] For slightly different versions of this verse, see Dulva, ix. fol. 36b (Bhixuni Prâtimoxa); Jatakanidânam, fol. 454b; and Fausböll's Jataka, p. 20, gâthâ 133, 134, *Yathapi camarî vâlam*, &c.

[4] Comp. Khaggavisânasutta (Sutta Nipata), 19.

creatures (bhuta), who is merciful to creatures, there never arises any ill feeling in him.[1]

43.

He who knows no evil thoughts, who is kind to all creatures, who is merciful to all living beings, there never arises any ill feeling in him.

44.

He who knows no evil thoughts, who is kind to creatures, who shows mercy to all sentient beings, there never arises any ill feeling in him.

45.

(Repetition of verse 44.)

46.

He who is kind to all his acquaintances, to all his friends, and to all creatures, and who entertains a spirit of mercy, will greatly increase his happiness.[2]

47.

If one has but thoughts devoid of cruelty for living beings, and shows mercy, he is by this fact virtuous; if one shows a compassionate heart to all sentient beings, he will attain such merit as is acquired by the elect (ariya).

48.

The man who with a joyous mind, without faintheartedness, observes the laws of virtue,[3] will arrive at perfection and happiness.

49.

Emancipated by perfect knowledge, he is safe and at

---

[1] Or it may be translated "there never arises ill-feeling toward him."

[2] He will either be born in the world of Brahma, or he will have the happiness of no harm (befalling him), or the happiness of reaching the end (of worldly life?)—P.

[3] Morality and meditation.—P.

rest; his mind being at rest, the actions of his body and his words are quiet.[1]

50.

Thus, by having the mind fixed on one point, one obtains perfect comprehension of the law, but it is not by having cymbals on the five limbs that one will find joy.

51.

They whose minds delight in meditation find no enjoyment in desires; he who is shielded from the smallest affliction will enjoy blissful slumber.

52.

They whose minds delight in meditation find no enjoyment in desires; he who is troubled by no affliction whatever will find great joy.

53.

He whose mind, like a rock, remains without being moved, who in the midst of passions is without passions, in the midst of anger is without anger, with a mind such as this it is not possible to experience suffering.

54 (185).

Speak no abuse, do no harm, be firm in the observance of the Pratimoxa, know how to be moderate in your food, take up your abode in a remote forest, and you will find peace of mind in spiritual insight (vipaçyana); this is the doctrine of the Buddha.[2]

---

[1] There is evidently a hiatus in the text of the Bkah-hgyur between the last line of verse 48 and the second line of verse 50. The text of the 71st vol. of the Bstan-hgyur gives, however, the missing lines, and it is from it that I have taken verse 49 and the first line of 50. These three verses were spoken on seeing King Adjatasatru amusing himself with his wives and court, and on hearing the inhabitants of Râjagriha exclaim on seeing him, "This is happiness! this is joy!" The latter part of verse 50 alludes most likely to the singers and dancers of the king.

[2] According to one account, there was at Çravasti a great concourse of Bhixus, who, on seeing a dead dog which omitted a most offensive odour, spoke evil words, some of them say-

55.

He who possesses a correct estimation of the mind, who appreciates the flavour of perfect solitude, protected by the earnestness of his meditative mind, he enjoys the pleasure of being without anything (that causes suffering).

56.

He whose attentive mind delights in the truth and adheres to the (four) truths,[1] who always walks in the way with his body, he is safe in speech and in mind,[2] and, casting off sorrow, he will experience no more suffering.

57.

He whose mind is not guarded, who is under the rule of false theories, subdued by sleep and laziness, he will fall into the power of Mâra.

58.

His mind therefore guarded, led by orthodox opinions, with perfect understanding in his way of doing,[3] perfectly comprehending birth and decay, the Bhixu, subduing sleep and laziness, has found the way to put an end to suffering.

59.

He who is pure is in safety; he whose mind is subdued and perfectly controlled is happy; all those who have been led astray by brutish instincts [4] will go to hell.

---

ing, "Who can have thrown this into the king's highway!" But the ayuchmat Ananda spoke extolling it—"Its teeth are white like a white rose," &c., he said.—P. Compare chap. xxxii. 30.

[1] There is some uncertainty in the first line. The text of the Bkah-hgyur reads *dben*, "solitude," in both cases; that of the Bst. *dben* and *bden*, "truth." The Comm. reads *bden* in both cases. I have followed this version.

[2] He is not exposed to lying, covetousness, &c.—P.

[3] Knowing the way to salvation (niryanika), &c.—P.

[4] *Skye-dgu sems kyis.* The Comm. explains *skye-dgu* by *srog-tchags*, "living being," but makes no other remark on this expression. It evidently implies such thoughts as are inherent to one's lower nature, as the Comm. speaks of the "fools who have a low (*thu-mal*) nature."

60.

He who is pure is in safety; he whose mind is subdued and perfectly controlled is happy; all those who have been led astray by brutish instincts will exist (hereafter) among beasts.

61.

He who is pure is in safety; he whose mind is subdued and perfectly controlled is happy; all those who have been led astray by brutish instincts will exist (hereafter) among pretas.

62.

He who is pure is in safety; he whose mind is subdued and perfectly controlled is happy; all those who are guarded against brutish instincts will find joy among men.

63.

He who is pure is in safety; he whose mind is subdued and perfectly controlled is happy; all those who are guarded against brutish instincts will find joy in heaven.

64.

He who is pure is in safety; he whose mind is subdued and perfectly controlled is happy; all those who are guarded against brutish instincts will find nirvâna.[1]

Chapter on the Mind, the Thirty-first.

---

[1] The last six verses were spoken for the following reason; Virudhaka, for having killed a great number of the Çakyas and delighting in killing, had been born in hell. The murdered Çakyas went on the happy way and left behind all sorrow. —P.

XXXII.

THE BHIXU.

1 (365).

A Bhixu who is satisfied with what alms are given him, and who frets not about what is given to others, who is protected by continual passionlessness and reflection, him the gods do delight in.

2.

A Bhixu who is satisfied with what alms are given him, and who frets not about what is given to others, who is protected (by passionlessness and reflection), and in whom the gods delight, in such a one there is no desire for honours, riches, and fame.

3.

A Bhixu who has cast off all desires, is free from passions, though having before him (the objects of desire); the steadfast one, who is without selfishness and is controlled, ought not to hold intercourse with others.[1]

4.

Hurt by the words of uncontrolled men, and listening to the words of the ill-natured, the Bhixu is without anger

---

[1] Çariputra having gone to the house of some relatives, had done them the kindness to teach them the law. An inimical Brahman, who could not bear it, said, "He has been deluded himself and does delude others." (Bhagavat) then said: "By entering the priesthood one cuts off desires which pervade all the regions of the world, one cuts off desires entirely. The Bixhu overcomes all that inwardly disturbs him by keeping his mind remote from all; by being in seclusion he can destroy the remotest root of desire—that is to say, the six vanities (*phra-rgyas*) of existence.—P.

what ere occurs, like the elephant pierced by arrows on the battlefield.

5.

Hurt by words of uncontrolled men, and listening to the words of the ill-natured, the Bhixu is equally composed what ere occurs, like the elephant pierced by arrows on the battlefield.

6.

Not exercising any handicraft [1] for the gratification of the self, his senses under control, perfectly emancipated, without fondness for a home, without selfishness, having cast off desires and living all alone, that man is a Bhixu.[2]

7 (375).

Associating only with men whose lives are pure and who are without slothfulness, observing the different prescriptions,[3] one will learn the necessary rules to follow in life (to acquire nirvâna).

8 (362).

He who controls his hands, who controls his feet, who controls his speech, who controls his senses, who finds all his pleasure in solitude, who is contented, him I call a Bhixu.

9 (364).

The Bhixu who finds perfect joy in the law, who delights in the law, who meditates on the law, who bears in mind the law, will never depart from the law.

10 (373).

The Bhixu having entered an empty abode [4] and seeing

---

[1] This is to teach dislike for worldly goods.—P.

[2] That is to say, one who has found the destruction of suffering—P.

[3] *So-sor byo-bshah bya.* There are two kinds of *byo-bshah* (prescriptions):—1. The different prescriptions of the law. 2. The different prescriptions concerning objects (*zang-zing*). — P. The first probably alludes to the Prâtimoxa, the latter to the Vinaya. Comp. the Pâli text *santuṭṭhi pâtimokkha ca samvaro.*

[4] Who has taken up his abode in solitude.—P.

the innermost (part of the law), will experience divine joy on perceiving the law rightly.

11 (374).

As soon as he has rightly understood the creation and destruction of the skandhas, he will find joy and ravishment; the Bhixu filled with joy will find the way to put an end to suffering.

12.

As a rocky mountain is unshaken by the wind, so likewise the Bhixu who has put an end to passions is immovable.

13.

As a rocky mountain is unshaken by the wind, so likewise the Bhixu who has put an end to ignorance is immovable.

14.

As a rocky mountain is unshaken by the wind, so likewise the Bhixu who has put an end to selfishness is immovable.

15.

As a rocky mountain is unshaken by the wind, so likewise the Bhixu who has put an end to lust is immovable.

16.

As a rocky mountain is unshaken by the wind, so likewise the Bhixu who has put an end to affection is immovable.[1]

17.

He who is without worldly goods, who cares not for self, for whom there is no affliction in anything, he is called a Bhixu.

---

[1] Mâha Maudgalyayana's body had been dreadfully beaten by Gudashikhiyaka (sic); the Brahmans and householders having come to where he was, asked why he showed no agitation. (Bhagavat) then spoke verses 12–16.—P. This probably alludes to Maudgalyayana's death. See Spence Hardy, Manual, p.351; also xxix. 52, and note 2, p. 150.

18.

They who only beg of others must not be considered as Bhixus; they who are attached to the ways of the world [1] must not be considered as Bhixus.

19.

He who has cast off virtue [2] and vice,[3] who leads a life of holiness, who lives away from the society of men, he is called a Bhixu.

20.

The Bhixu who is kind, who has perfect faith in the teaching of the Buddha, will find the perfection of peace (amatam padam), of which one can never weary.

21.

The Bhixu who is kind, who has perfect faith in the teaching of the Buddha, will find the perfection of peace, the peace from the sanskâra (body).

22.

The Bhixu who is kind, who has perfect faith in the teaching of the Buddha, will arrive by degrees at the complete destruction of all attachment.

23.

The Bhixu who is kind, who has perfect faith in the teaching of the Buddha, will pull himself out of the evil way, as the elephant does himself out of the mire.[4]

24.

The Bhixu who is kind, who has perfect faith in the

---

[1] Lit. the practice (tchos) of the village, which the Commentary explains by selfishness.
[2] The fruits of existence.—P.
[3] Not desiring the fruits (hbras- bu ma hdod pao). I cannot explain these definitions as they are given in the Comment.
[4] Comp. Dhamm., 327, and iv. 26; also verses 24, 25, with iv. 27, 28.

teaching of the Buddha, will shake off all wickedness, as does the wind the leaves of a tree.

25.

The Bhixu who is kind, who has perfect faith in the teaching of the Buddha, is so near nirvâṇa that he cannot possibly fall away from it.[1]

26.

The Bhixu who has subdued what charms the heart, what is agreeable to the mind, what delights and what does not delight (*i.e.*, passions), is full of delight, and will find the end of suffering.

27.

His body at rest[2] and dispassionate, his mind perfectly composed, having cast off all worldly affairs, the Bhixu is (then) in peace, I declare.

28 (372).

Without meditation (samâdhi) there is no knowledge; without knowledge there is no meditation: he who possesses knowledge and meditation, he shall be called a Bhixu.[3]

29.

They who are wise devote themselves to meditation and knowledge; the first thing therefore for an intelligent Bhixu is to acquire these.

---

[1] The boatmen living on the shore of the Ganges, being angered, had commenced abusing Bhagavat and his disciples when yet a great way off. On drawing nigh, all the disciples remarked Bhagavat's perfectly calm exterior; so they, believing in him, requested him to go to these boatmen (and talk to them); having done which, he spoke to (his disciples) verses 20–25.—P.

[2] Having given up all wicked deeds.—P.

[3] A great number of Ashthavangana (*sic*) Rischis were assembled on the shore of the Ayoda (Ayôdhyâ?), and on seeing the Bhixus they were greatly pleased (with their appearance). Bhagavat spoke the two following verses (28, 29).—P. There is a slight difference in the last line of 28 between the text of the Bkah. and that of the Bst. According to the latter, it is "he is near to nirvâṇa." The Comment. follows the version of the Bst.

30.

Learn contentment and to control the senses; consider well what is necessary to salvation,[1] learn to be moderate in your food, live in a secluded spot, and seek peace of mind in spiritual insight (vipaçyana); this is the doctrine of the Buddha.[1]

31 (378).

He who has not sinned in either body, speech, or mind, his conduct is virtuous, his mind is chaste, he is a Bhixu.

32.

He who meditates on the seven constituent parts of sambodhi,[2] has the greatest of virtues, perfect composure, he is a Bhixu.

33.

He who in this world has learned how to put an end to his suffering, who is pure and wise and without corruption (âsrava), he is called a Bhixu.

34.

He who, though virtuous, or an ascetic, or one who has heard much, has not been able to put an end to sinfulness though he lives in solitude, if he becomes wearied of seeking to obtain samadhi, and gives it up through want of confidence, he is not a Bhixu.[3]

35.

The elements of being (skandha), that are called the individual, are the afflictions of this world; perfect en-

---

[1] Comp. xxxi. 54, and Dham., 185. Vipaçyana is here explained by "the four dhyanas of being without âsravas."

[2] See Burnouf, Lotus, p. 796 et seq.; Foucaux, Rgya tcher rol pa, p. 36; and Buddh. trigl., fol. 18a.

[3] This verse, spoken previously by the Buddha, was repeated by a Deva to a Bhixu who had devoted himself to a forest life, but had given up exerting himself, though he possessed great virtues. The following verse, that had been spoken by Bhagavat at Uruvilva, a short time after attaining buddhaship, was also repeated on this occasion.

lightenment (samyak sambodhi) is happiness; to it the elect must devote themselves.

36.

According to the way one has thought, so shall he become in another (life); they will come back again to this world, they who love existence, who delight in existence, who long for worldly goods, who consider but existence (in their theories), who delight in existence itself.

37.

Their joy is but suffering, their happiness but trembling with fear; they who would free themselves of existence, devote themselves to a life of purity (brahmacharya).

38.

Çramanas and Brahmans all do teach that existence is deliverance from existence;[1] they none of them know deliverance from existence, I declare.

39.

Çramanas and Brahmans all do teach that existence is deliverance from existence; they none of them know real emancipation from existence, I declare.

40.

Suffering is the outcome of attachment to existence[2] (upâdâna), and from suffering proceeds attachment: if all attachments are destroyed there will not be produced any more suffering.

---

[1] That is to say, the goal they offer to their followers—life in Brahmâ's heaven—is still a corporeal existence, which of course cannot be permanent.

[2] *Len-pa* = ñe-bar len-pa, "to seek for eagerly."—P. It is the ninth nidana. Burnouf translates this word by "conception." See Intr., p. 494.

41.

"To whatever form of existence one has attachment,[1] it is impermanent, miserable, subject to change;" he who by perfect knowledge regards them all in this light, will cast off all fondness for existence, and will find delight in the destruction of existence.[2]

42.

Then the Bhixu who has left sorrow behind (nibbuta) is safe, (for) being without attachment to another (existence), he will put an end to existence; subduing Mâra, conquering in the fight, he will then be delivered from all existences: this is the end of suffering.[3]

43.

The Bhixu who has cut himself off from existence (bhava), who is dispassionate, whose mind is at peace, will not experience existence again, having fallen out of the orb of regeneration.

44.

The Bhixu who has cut himself off from existence, who is dispassionate, whose mind is at peace, is freed from the bonds of Mâra, having fallen out of the orb of regeneration.

45.

The Bhixu who has cut himself off from existence, whose mind has become without sin (âsrava), will not experience existence again, having fallen out of the orb of regeneration.

46.

The Bhixu who has cut himself off from existence, whose mind has become without sin, is freed from the bonds of Mâra, having fallen out of the orb of regeneration.

---

[1] By upâdâna is meant the five upâdânaskandhas.—P.

[2] This udâna and the following one are in prose.

[3] These three verses are opposed to the opinions expressed in verses 38 and 39.

47.

The Bhixu who has cut himself off from existence, who has cut to pieces fondness for existence, will not experience existence again, and has fallen out of the orb of regeneration.

48.

The Bhixu who has cut himself off from existence, who has cut off fondness for existence, is freed from the bonds of Mâra, having fallen out of the orb of regeneration.[1]

49.

He who, having crossed the swamp (of desire), and being (no longer) pricked by the thorns of worldliness,[2] has found the way to put an end to passions, he is (truly) called a Bhixu.

50.

He who, having crossed the swamp, and being (no longer) pricked by the thorns of worldliness, has found the way to put an end to hatred, he is (truly) called a Bhixu.[3]

55.

He who has put an end[4] to reviling, killing, hurting, and to the thorns of worldliness, who is as immovable as a mountain, whom pleasure does not disturb, he is a Bhixu.

---

[1] In Kaushambi a great famine having come on, the Bhixus, their attention being diverted from alms-gathering (? *slong-mos gyengs-shing*), their bodies and minds became so dispassionate that they arrived at the comprehension of freedom (moxa). The famine having passed away, the six preceding verses were spoken to deter them from resuming their former habits (of devoting themselves solely to gathering alms).—P. Comp. Beal, *loc. cit.*, p. 53.

[2] Lit., "thorns of the town," that is, desire of profit, honours, &c.—P.

[3] Verses 51–54 are the same as 49, 50, without "ignorance, selfishness, lust, affection," in the place of "hatred."

[4] *Thul-ba*, "to allay" (the dust); "hurting," literally, "to bind, to put in bondage."

56.

The Bhixu who does not revile or exaggerate,[1] who perceives that this world is like a mirage, casts off what is and is not of the other shore, as a snake shuffles off its old worn-out skin.

57.

As the physician cures the poison of the snake, so the Bhixu who conquers rising passions casts off what is and is not of the other shore, as a snake shuffles off its old worn-out skin.[2]

64.

The Bhixu who eradicates every particle of the passions as does the mighty river the weak embankment, casts off what is and is not of the other shore, as a snake shuffles off its old worn-out skin.[3]

70.

The Bhixu who casts off all the qualities of desire, who frees himself from all the bonds of holding on to desire, casts off what is and is not of the other shore, as a snake shuffles off its old worn-out skin.[4]

71.

The Bhixu who, having cast off all mental obscurities, is without sin, whose mind is severed from the grief of misery, casts off what is and is not of the other shore, as a snake shuffles off its old worn-out skin.

---

[1] *Sgro-hdogs.* There is much uncertainty about the proper way of rendering this word. See Jäschke, s.v. *sgro.* The Comment. does not allude to it. As to the first verb, it says, "We must not revile, not seeing that all conditions (dharma) are, by their nature, nothing." "These two (reviling and exaggerating) are to teach to cast off any low habits."

Comp. Uragasutta (Sutta Nipata), 6.

[2] Comp. Uragasutta, 11. Verses 58-63 similar to this one, substituting for "passions," "hatred, ignorance, selfishness, lust, anger, affections."

[3] Verses 65-69 like this one, substituting for "passions," "hatred, ignorance, selfishness, lust, affection."

[4] Comp. Uragasutta, 16.

72.

The Bhixu whose judgment is clear, who sees clearly into everything, casts off what is and is not of the other shore, as a snake shuffles off its old worn-out skin.

73.

The Bhixu who has eradicated the whole forest of sinfulness, casts off what is and is not of the other shore, as a snake shuffles off its old worn-out skin.

74.

The Bhixu who has eradicated all the plagues, &c.,[1] of sinfulness, casts off what is and is not of the other shore, as a snake shuffles off its old worn-out skin.

75.

The Bhixu who has eradicated every sinful inclination,[2] casts off what is and is not of the other shore, as a snake shuffles off its old worn-out skin.

76.

The Bhixu who observes the law, who is in contemplation (dhyâna) of the void (of all substances), who has continual peace of mind,[3] who has left sorrow behind (nibbuta), is happy.

77.

The Bhixu who, speaking neither pleasantly nor unpleasantly, takes up his abode in remote places, living in purity, entirely drives out love of existence and (sinful) inclinations.

Chapter on the Bhixu, the Thirty-second.

---

[1] Such as anger, &c.—P.

[2] Or *bags* (or *bag*) *la ñal ba = phra rgyas*, "temptations." They comprise affections, passions, selfishness, ignorance, doubt, &c. See also Wassilieff, Buddh., p. 24 note. They are 98 or 118 in number, he says.

[3] Who is a yogin; this term is nearly a synonym of dhyâna.

XXXIII.

THE BRÂHMANA.

1 (142).

He who, though having ornamental apparel, is righteous, controlled, quiet, restrained, leading a life of holiness (brahmacharya), who neither harms or kills any living thing, he is a Brâhmana, a Çramana, he is a Bhixu.[1]

2 (141).

It is not by nakedness, by long hair, by dirt, by fasting, or by sleeping on the bare ground, not by dust and dirt,[2] or by devoting oneself to sitting motionless, that men become pure and leave their doubts behind.

3.

Whatever Çramanas and Brâhmanas there be who have passions, they will not put an end to sinfulness (the âsravas), and will experience the suffering of passing from life to life[3] (transmigrating).

---

[1] "Brâhmana" means one who has cast off sin, one who has many good qualities, who does not suffer from desires, who walks in the way; "Çramana," one who has quieted sin, or who practises virtue; "Bhixu," one who has conquered corruption (kleça), or one who is held by the prescriptions of the Pratimoxa.—P.

[2] *Rdul dang dri-ma*. *Rdul* means "ashes," and *dri-ma* means "dust" (*rdul*), and any other small particles of dirt.—P. Comp. Burnouf, Introd., pp. 324, 325, where these two verses occur in the Legend of Sangha Raxchita, taken from the Divya Avadâna.

[3] *Bar-ma-dor, hkhor-bai nang duo*. According to Tibetan ideas, *bar-ma do* means "the intermediate state between death and rebirth, of a shorter or longer duration (yet not of more than forty days), &c. See Jäschke, s.v., and Schlaginweit, Buddh. in Tibet, p. 109.

4.

Whatever Çramanas and Brâhmanas there be who have passions, they will not put an end to sensation (vedanâ), and will experience the suffering of passing from life to life.

5.

Whatever Çramanas and Brâhmanas there be who have passions, and who have but a foolish object in view,[1] they will experience the suffering of passing from life to life.

6.

Whatever Çramanas and Brâhmanas there be who have passions,[2] the foolish, stupid men will experience the suffering of passing from life to life.

7.

Whatever Çramanas and Brâhmanas there be who have passions, they will not find the blessed ideal (nirvâna), and will experience the suffering of passing from life to life.

8 (394).

O fool! what is the use of thy long locks? what is the use of thy garment of skin? Within thee there abides darkness; the outside thou makest clean.[3]

9 (393).

One does not become a Brâhmana by his family, by his

---

[1] The satisfying of their desires, the acquisition of wealth, &c.—P.

[2] Thinking that existence can be the final deliverance from existence.—P. See chap. xxxii. 38.

[3] There lived in a house on the shore of the Valgumata (sic) river a young Brahman, who having wrapped around his person stuff (ras) that resembled long hair, was deceiving men. Bhagavat having heard of him, came that way, and converted him.—P. Comp. the Kuhakabrâhmana (deceitful Brahman) in Fausböll's Dham., v. 394, p. 427.

long locks, by his lineage; he who possesses the law of truth and who is pure, he is a Brâhmana.

10.

One does not become a Brâhmana by his family, by his long locks, by his lineage; he who casts away all sins both great and small, him, because he has cast away sin, I call a Brâhmana.

11.

A man is not a Çramana on account of his shaven head, a man is not a Brâhmana because he says "Om!"[1] He who knows what is virtue, and who is pure, he is a Brâhmana.

12.

A man is not a Çramana on account of his shaven head; a man is not a Brâhmana because he says "Om!" He who casts away all sins both great and small, he, because he has cast away sins, is a Çramana, a Brâhmana.

13.

One does not become pure by washing, as do the common of mortals in this world; he who casts away every sin both great and small, he, because he has cast away sins, is a Çramana, a Brâhmana.[2]

14.

He who has cast off all sinfulness, who devotes himself to continual reflection, who has the perfect enlightenment of the destruction of all attachment, he in the (three) worlds is a Brâhmana.[3]

---

[1] Om! *i.e.*, "om, bhur, bhavah, svah." The pronouncing of these syllables does not constitute a Brâhman, for a magpie can repeat them also.—P.

[2] Bhagavat was living at the stûpa of Gayâçira when at the time of the feast of the summer month (*dpyid zlar-bai*) many hundreds of thousand people came there to bathe and be cleansed of their sins; then it was that Bhagavat spoke this verse.—P.

[3] A Brahman called Puskarâsira (*sic*) said to Bhagavat, "Venerable one! as the all-knowing elephant is

15.

The Brâhmana who has cast off all sinfulness, who is without hypocrisy, and who leads a pure life, has reached the perfection (set forth in) the Vedas;[1] his life is a life of holiness (brahmacharya), and when he does speak, his speech is holy.

16.

He who is not given to deceiving, who is without selfishness, who is without passions, without expectation, who has conquered hatred, who is on the way to nirvâna (the extinction of sorrow), he is a Brâhmana, a Çramana, he is a Bhixu.

17 (396).

He who has been born of woman, if he has great possessions, he may be called "Bhovadi,"[2] but I call him not a Brâhmana; he who possesses nothing, who accepts nothing, him I call a Brâhmana.

18 (391).

He who does nothing sinful in body, speech, and mind, who has the three parts well controlled, he, I declare, is a Brâhmana.

19.

He who uses not harsh words, who speaks what is right (true) and pleasing, who is without sinfulness, he, I declare, is a Brâhmana.

---

the first among elephants, the thoroughbred horse the first among horses, the wish-tree (a tree that grants every wish) the first among trees, a jewel (ratna) the first among treasures, so likewise, Venerable one, Çramanas and Brahmans are the best, and the greatest among men."—P. See on the wish-tree, Beal, Romantic Legend, p. 258; also Gubernatis, Mythologie des Plantes, and Schiefner's Tibetan Tales, p. 9.

[1] *Rig-byed mthar-phyin.* The goal of the Vedas being the destruction of vedanâ, the saint (*mthar-phyin-pa*) of the Veda is a living being.—P. This verse teaches, in other words, the destruction of passions. The Comment. is not very satisfactory.

[2] *De ming bhu dses smra-bar bstan.* One who uses bhur, bhu, &c., may be called by that name. —P. Compare the Pâli *bhovadi nâma so hoti*. See also Childers, J. R. A. S., new series, v. p. 230, and Dict., s.v. *bho;* also Sutta Nipata, 620.

20 (399).

He who patiently endures stripes,[1] bonds, and abuse, in whose manner is patience, which gives the strength of a host,[2] he, I declare, is a Brâhmana.

21 (400).

He who is without anger, who observes the precepts, well-behaved, without desires, who has now a body for the last time, he, I declare, is a Brâhmana.

22 (404).

He who no longer dwells among either the clergy or the laity, who has few desires, who frequents not houses, he, I declare, is a Brâhmana.

23.

He for whom there are no pleasures in the future, who feels no pain on account of those he has left behind, who has thrown off the bond of voluptuousness, who has conquered in the fight (against Mâra), he, I declare, is a Brâhmana.

24.

He for whom there are no pleasures in the future, who feels no pain on account of those he has left behind, who is immaculate, dispassionate, without sorrow, he, I declare, is a Brâhmana.

---

[1] *Gsod*, lit. "to cut, to kill." Comp. the Pâli *vadho*.

[2] *Bzod-pai brtul-dsugs stobs tsogs chan*, literally "of patience the manner, strength, having a multitude." The Comment. explains *tsogs* by *dpung*, "an army." "If a king has an army (*dpung-gi tsogs*) composed of the four (necessary) elements, he cannot be conquered by others, but will vanquish others. In like manner, he whose manner is patient can, after having overcome sin, be victorious also of the three worlds.—P. Compare what Childers says of the word *balâniko*, s.v. This verse was spoken on account of Baradhvadja abusing Bhagavat from as far off as he could see him. —P.

25.

He who nourishes not the smallest desire, who is subdued, who is devoted to (acquiring) the chief thing (nirvâṇa), who has destroyed sinfulness (âsravas), who is cleansed from stains, he, I declare, is a Brâhmana.

26 (385).

He for whom there is neither this side nor that side, who has reached the end of all conditions,[1] he, I declare, is a Brâhmana.

27.

He for whom there is neither this side or that side, who is without fondness for the three objects,[2] he, I declare, is a Brâhmana.

28 (409).

He who takes nothing in this world, whether it be short or long, thin or thick, good or bad, he, I declare, is a Brâhmana.[3]

29.

He then who, having wisdom, puts an end to his suffering, being without passions, free from everything, he, I declare, is a Brâhamana.

30.

He who has cast off both virtue and vice, who is di-

---

[1] Who has reached the other shore of the twelve âyatanas.—P. The twelve âyatanas are the six organs of sense and the six objects of sense.

[2] The twelve âyatanas and the self.—P.

[3] In the Dandaki forest there dwelt two Brahmans, who, devoting themselves to (practising) long and short periods of asceticism and to wearing long and short garments, were considered by the people to be Brâhmanas. Bhagavat coming to where they were, they asked him, "Gautama, whom do you consider as a Brâhmana?" He then answered the four following verses (28-31). They then threw away their long and short garments, their trifling (lit. thin) and roughness (thick), their finery (? *mdzes-pa*), and having entered the priesthood, they became free from passions.—P. I may not have perfectly understood the latter part of the last phrase of the Comment., but the general sense is quite clear.

vested of everything, who is without passion (râga), at peace, he, I declare, is a Brâhmana.

31.

He who has left behind all fondness for virtue and vice, who has left fondness behind, who is perfectly emancipated, he, I declare, is a Brâhmana.

32.

He for whom there is no behind, before, and between, who is without passion (râga), freed from bondage, he, I declare, is a Brâhmana.[1]

33.

He who, like water on the leaf of a lotus, like a mustard seed on the end of a reed,[2] does not adhere to vice, he, I declare, is a Brâhmana.

34 (401).

He who, like water on the leaf of a lotus, like a mustard seed on the end of a reed, does not adhere to pleasures, he, I declare, is a Brâhmana.

35.

He who, like water on the leaf of a lotus, like a mustard seed on the end of a reed, has thrown off delight in existence, he, I declare, is a Brâhmana.

36.

He who, like the moon, is chaste, pure, undefiled, per-

---

[1] "Behind" refers to the period during which the present mendicant led a householder's life; "before" (or "afterwards") to the period at which he commenced the life of a recluse (âranyaka); "between" (or "intermediate") to the period during which he was overcoming all worldliness.—P.

[2] As a mustard seed cannot remain on the end of a reed if its centre has been bored out, so likewise sins and anger (drop off) from him who has (once) cast them away. — P. "Vice," he goes on to say, means "desires" (trichnâ).

fectly clear, who has stripped off sinfulness, he, I declare is a Brâhmana.

37 (413).

He who, like the moon, is chaste, pure, undefiled, perfectly clear, who has cast off all delight in existence, he, I declare, is a Brâhmana.

38.

He who is stripped [1] of sinfulness, as is the heaven of mire and the moon of dust, he, I declare, is a Brâhmana.

39.

He who is stripped of desires, as is the heaven of mire and the moon of dust, he, I declare, is a Brâhmana.

40.

He who has cast off all delight in existence, as does the heaven mire and the moon dust, he, I declare, is a Brâhmana.

41.

He who dwells (in solitude), free from passion (râga), meditating, without sin (âsrava), having done what ought to be done,[2] subdued, having his last body, he, I declare, is a Brâhmana.

42 (403).

He whose knowledge is deep, whose mind is well directed, who knows the right and the wrong way, who has found the greatest blessing (the way to nirvâna), he, I declare, is a Brâhmana.

43.

The men, whoever they be, who live solely on alms, who have nothing that is their own, who do no harm, who are

---

[1] *Mi gos-de*, literally "not robed with."

[2] Having found out the way, and freed himself of the three evil ways. —P.

steadfast, who live a life of holiness (brahmatcharya), who, being perfectly wise (themselves), teach the law (the nidânas), they, I declare, are Brâhmanas.

44 (415).

He who casts off desires, who becomes homeless on entering the priesthood, who puts an end to the sin of desire, he, I declare, is a Brâhmana.

45.

He who does not harm any living creature, who does not kill or take part in killing, he, I declare, is a Brâhmana.

46.

He who is tolerant with the intolerant, who patiently endures punishment, who is merciful to all creatures, he, I declare, is a Brâhmana.

47 (407).

As a mustard seed on the point of a reed (drops off), so he who keeps passions, hatred, and selfishness under control, he, I declare, is a Brâhmana.

48.

He who passes beyond this stronghold of affections and the river of transmigration, who having crossed over (*i.e.*, having found the way to nirvâna), has not both his mind and thoughts preoccupied about going to the other shore, who has left behind attachment (upâdâna), he, I declare, is a Brâhmana.

49 (410).

He who has no desire for this world or for the other, who has put an end to all fondness for existence, he, I declare, is a Brâhmana.

50.

He who is without love for this world or for the other, who is without love, who has completely cast it off, he, I declare, is a Brâhmana.

51.

He who, casting off what is pleasant and unpleasant, has become cool (*i.e.*, has found contentment), who is without sin, who has overcome the whole world, who is steadfast, he, I declare, is a Brâhmana.

52 (417).

He who, having cast off human attachment,[1] has left behind the attachment of the gods, he who is free from all attachment, he, I declare, is a Brâhmana.

53 (420).

He whose way the Devas, Gandharvas, and men comprehend not, he whose passiveness mankind does not comprehend, he, I declare, is a Brâhmana.

54.

He for whom there exists no law that is not known and understood, he who sees to the remotest parts of knowledge, he, I declare, is a Brâhmana.

55 (423).

He who, knowing his former abodes (existences), perceives heaven (svarga) and hell, the Muni who has found the way to put an end to birth, who is perfected in knowledge, who knows the termination of suffering, he, I declare, is a Brâhmana.

56.

He whose mind is perfectly emancipated, who is wise,

---

[1] *Sbyor*, in Pâli *yoga*. Prof. Max Müller's translation of this verse does not agree with this or with M. Fausböll's translation.

who is delivered from all passions, who possesses the triple knowledge[1] (trividyâ), he, I declare, is a Brâhmana.

57 (419).

He who understands the deaths, changes, and births of all sentient creatures, who has the all-penetrating eye (sammanta chakkhu), who is perfectly enlightened (Buddha), he, I declare, is a Brâhmana.

58.

He who has left all attachment behind, who is without affliction, without joy, who is reflective, and who teaches (others), he, I declare, is a Brâhmana.

59 (422).

He who is a Muni, a conqueror (djina), the greatest of Rischis, the chief of chiefs,[2] the greatest of bulls[3] (usabham), who has nought to seek for, who has been washed clean, who is perfectly enlightened (Buddha), he, I declare, is a Brâhmana.

60.

He who has given up existence, who has conquered everything, who has crossed the stream, who is well away (from the world), who has cast off everything, and has reached the other shore, he, I declare, is a Brâhmana.

61.

He who thinks not of what is sinful, who does not speak inconsiderately, who lives, his mind free from passion, (râga), he, I declare, is a Brâhmana.

---

[1] To be able to remember one's former conditions, to know the thoughts of others, to have supernatural knowledge (abhidjnâ).—P. See Foucaux, Rgya tcher rol-pa, p. 336, transl.

[2] *Khyu - mtchog = richabha*, according to the Mahâvyutpatti, ch. 1.

[3] *Glang-po tche*, "having the perfect qualities of Mahesvara."—P. All the qualities alluded to in this verse and in the two preceding ones are generally applied to Bhagavat himself.

62.

He whose clothes come from piles of rubbish, who learns to be modest, who is without desires, who lives near a tree, he, I declare, is a Brâhmana.

63.

He who, having cast away all suffering, is at rest, and who gives himself up to meditating on the holy eightfold way, he, I declare, is a Brâhmana.

64.

He who has given up everything (worldly), who is enlightened, without doubt and misery, who perceives the perfect state free from death (akkhara?—*i.e.*, nirvâna), he, I declare, is a Brâhmana.

65.

He who is without a body,[1] who lives in a cave, who wanders about alone, who controls the fleeting mind which is hard to control, he, I declare, is a Brâhmana.

66.

He who comprehends the immaterial (arûpa) which cannot be seen, the infinite (ananta) which cannot possibly be seen, the subtle, the fundamental,[2] who is always reflective, who has put an end to all attachment (yoga), who is perfectly enlightened (Buddha), he, in this world, is a Brâhmana.

67.

He who has destroyed the fastenings (?) and the cords,[3]

---

[1] *Lus-med*, without form (rûpa).—P. It may mean "without care for the body." "This verse is to teach that he whose mind is controlled finds nirvâna."—P.

[2] "These epithets apply to nir-"vâna." "Subtile," because the senses have been left behind.—P.

[3] *Sogs-mig* and *tchings-ma*. As when the load is fastened on the waggon and the fastenings (*sogs-mig*) and cords (*tchings-ma*) are in place the load cannot be thrown off, so he who cuts the fastenings (*i.e.*, affections), and the cords (*i.e.*, ignorance), can throw off the suffering of transmigration. *Tchings-ma* is "a wooden peg." *Sogs-mig* I am unable to explain satisfactorily, unless it be a hole in which the peg is inserted to hold the load together.

who by cutting the cords and the ropes has thrown off all affliction and is enlightened, he, I declare, is a Brâhmana.

68.

He who has destroyed desires for (worldly) goods, sinfulness, the bonds of the eye of the flesh, who has torn up desire by the very root, he, I declare, is a Brâhmana.

69.

He who by earnestness has cut the stream, who has overcome all desires, who knows the end of the sanskâra, who is without sin, he is a Brâhmana.

70 (294).

He who has killed father and mother and two pure (çuxi) kings, and who has conquered their kingdoms with the inhabitants, is without sin, is a Brâhmana.

71 (295).

He who has killed father and mother and two pure kings, and who has killed an irresistible tiger[1] (veyyaggha, *i.e.*, cruelty), is without sin, is a Brâhmana.

72 (389).

He who stupidly drives away a virtuous Brâhmana, is wicked; one should not strike Brâhmanas; one should not drive away Brâhmanas.

---

[1] *Stag*, "tiger," implies a being whose mind is solely bent on evil. As the tiger in its natural ferocity devours unhesitatingly flesh and blood, so likewise, he whose mind is bent on evil or spitefulness devours all the roots of virtue (that appear in others?). The five (persons killed) imply the five mental darknesses.—P. The five mental darknesses or *panchakachâya* (Pâli *pancakilesa*) are lust, ignorance, pride, shamelessness, and hardness of heart, or, according to Clough, lust, anger, ignorance, self-confidence, and pride. See Childers, s.v. Pâñcakilesani, and Burnouf, Lotus, p. 360. The Tibetan Comment. does not explain this term. In both this verse and the preceding one we might translate the second line by "a king and two pure men." This would agree with the Chinese version, which is very obscure, as M. Beal has informed me.

73.

He who perfectly understands the laws should be honoured and respected by both young and old, as the Brâhmana does the holy fire (aggihuttam).

74.

He who perfectly understands the laws should be honoured and reverentially approached by both old and young, as does the Brâhmana the holy fire.

75 (392).

He who perfectly understands the law taught by the perfect Buddha, should be honoured and respected, as the Brâhmana does the holy fire.

76.

He who perfectly understands the law taught by the perfect Buddha should be honoured and reverentially approached, as does the Brâhmana the holy fire.

77.

When the Brâhmana has reached the other shore of existence, then he stands alone, having left far behind (all fear) of Piçâtchas (and Râkchas like) Vakula.[1]

78.

When the Brâhmana has reached the other shore of existence (lit. of the law), then he sees, and all the perceptions (vedanâ [2]) vanish from his sight.

79.

When the Brâhmana has reached the other shore

---

[1] Vakula was the name of a Râkcha who was greatly tormenting the inhabitants of Magadha. The verse, however, is obscure.

[2] The vedanâ of holding on to existence are at an end.—P.

of existence, then he sees, and all causes [1] (hetu) vanish.

80.

When the Brâhmana has reached the other shore of existence, then he sees, and all attachment (yoga) vanishes.

81.

When the Brâhmana has reached the other shore of existence, then he leaves behind him birth, old age, and death.

82 (387, 1st part).

The sun shines by day, the moon shines by night, the suit of armour of the king doth shine,[2] the Brâhmana shines in his meditation.

83 (387, 2d part).

The sun shines by day, the moon shines by night, continually, day and night, does the luminous (form of the) Buddha shine.

84.

As Brâhmanas and the like have left behind everything that is disagreeable, as my mind has consequently left behind (all passions), I have truly put an end to all pettiness.[3]

85.

When the ardent, meditative Brâhmana has perfectly understood the (different) conditions (dharma) and their causes (the twelve nidânas), and when these ideas have

---

[1] There being no causes there are no fruits (effects).—P.

[2] Or "the king shines in his suit of armour."

[3] Bhagavat was living at Râjagriha in the grove of Amrâpâli, when Adjatasatru came to him and said: "Venerable one, I have done thee frequently great wrong, and by befriending thy wicked kinsman (Dêvadatta) I have committed great evil. I pray thee have mercy on me a sinner (and forgive me)."— P. "Pettiness" implies here bearing any ill-will towards the king for his past wickedness.

become perfectly clear to him, then he casts away every particle of perplexity.

86.

When the ardent, meditative Brâhmana has perfectly understood suffering and its cause, and when this idea (dharma) has become perfectly clear to him, then he casts away every particle of perplexity.

87.

When the ardent, meditative Brâhmana has discovered the destruction of sensation (vedanâ), and when this idea has become perfectly clear to him, then he casts away every particle of perplexity.

88.

When the ardent, meditative Brâhmana has discovered the cessation of all causes (hetu), and (when) this idea has become perfectly clear to him, then he casts away every particle of perplexity.[1]

89.

When the ardent, meditative Brâhmana has discovered the cessation of sinfulness (âsravas), and when this idea has become perfectly clear to him, then he casts away every particle of perplexity.

90.

When to the ardent, meditative Brâhmana all these ideas have become perfectly clear, he stands lighting up all the worlds (or the whole world) as the sun illuminates the sky.

91.

When to the ardent, meditative Brâhmana, who by

---

[1] Comp. Mahâvagga, i. 1, 5.

knowledge has become emancipated from all attachment (yoga), all these ideas have become perfectly clear, he stands, having dispelled the hosts of Mâra (like the sun that illuminates the sky?).[1]

Chapter on the Brâhmana, the Thirty-third.

The Udânavarga compiled by Dharmatrâta is finished.

Translated (into Tibetan) by the Indian Pandit Vidyaprabhakara[2] and the Lotsâva Bande-rin-tchen-mtchog; revised and arranged by the corrector, the Lotsâva Bande-dpal-brtsegs.

---

[1] These last two verses are to be found condensed into one in the Mahâvagga, i. 1, 7. P. says that the last seven verses were spoken by Bhagavat "while sitting cross-legged at the foot of the Bodhi tree uninterruptedly for seven days," &c. The account he gives is exactly the same as that given in the Mahâvagga.

[2] According to the text of the seventy-first volume of the Bstan-hgyur, and also Schmidt's Index der Kandjur, pp. 42, 46, and 50, his name is Vidyakaraprabha, and this, I think, is the correct reading. In the seventy-first volume of the Bst., at the end of the text of the Udâna, I find the following note: "This (work) contains 1540 çlokas." I am unable to explain this, unless we consider a çloka as composed of four lines, each one separated by a *tchad*, in the prose parts as well as in the versified ones, and in that case we might possibly be able to divide the text into about that number of çlokas.

APPENDIX.

Verse 5, ch. i. p. 2.

"*Those pigeon-coloured bones,*" &c.

There were at Çravasti some newly-ordained Bhixus who were given to anger, to dress, to wearing jewels, &c., considering the body of paramount importance and caring nought for reading and hearing (the Scriptures). Bhagavat, on account of their sinfulness, went with them into a cemetery. It happened that at that time the bones of five hundred robbers had been cast away there. Bhagavat, drawing nigh, spoke as follows: "Look, Bhixus; may these bones of the dead fill you with awe, and teach you to shun regeneration, and to see the value of worldly goods."

Verse 21, ch. i. p. 4.

"*It is the law of humanity,*" &c.

A sea-captain had gone to sea for the seventh time, and had gathered together many jewels, &c., but a short time after he had reached his home with all this shining heap, he died. The king then confiscated all his widow's treasures, and she died shortly afterwards through grief (at her loss), and this was the origin (nidâna) of this gâtha.

Verse 22, ch. i. p. 4.

"*The end of all that has been hoarded up*," &c.

Four merchants of Çravasti considered (the first one), riches as the greatest blessing of life, (the second), houses, (the third), meeting his friends, (the fourth), the elixir of life. The king confiscated the riches of the first, the houses of the second were burnt up, the third lost his friends, and the fourth died. Bhagavat on hearing this spoke this udâna.

Verse 7, ch. viii. p. 37.

"*They whose minds are perverted*," &c.

"Dêvadatta, casting off the way taught by Bhagavat, was teaching that the five following fundamental rules were (necessary) to lead to the truth (paramârtha): 1. Not to make use of milk as a drink, for by so doing it harmed the calf; 2. not to eat meat, for by so doing sentient creatures were hurt; 3. not to cut off fringes (kha tsar), for it impaired the work of the weaver; 4. not to make use of salt; 5. not to live in forests, for it deprived the charitable of the merit of making alms."

This account of the first schism in Buddhism is quite different from what is told by Spence Hardy and Bigandet. Dêvadatta's five propositions, according to them, were: 1. To live in forests; 2. to eat only such food as they had collected themselves; 3. to wear only robes made of rags; 4. to abstain from fish and meat; 5. to dwell in unroofed places.

Hiuen Thsang saw in the kingdom of Karnasuvarna three convents occupied by followers of Dêvadatta, and who used neither milk nor butter (Si-yu-ki, x. p. 85). Fah-Hian says, in speaking of the kingdom of Kosala, " Dêvadatta also has a body of disciples still existing;

they pay religious reverence to the three past Buddhas, but not to Sakyamuni.[1]

I have not been able to explain the reason why salt was not used. The text is: "*Lan-tsa bzah-bar mi bya-ste, dbang-phyung-tchen-pir khu-ba* (or *za*) *las yang-dag-par hbyung-bai phyir-ro.*"

It appears likely that on the fifth proposition, the Tibetan Comment must be wrong. As to the others, they may be made to agree, to a certain extent, with those given elsewhere.

Verses 1, 2, ch. ix. p. 39.

"*He gives up the one great rule,*" &c.

The Ayuchmat Rahula was residing in a monastery at Râjagriha to perform penance, when Bhagavat came there to instruct him. Seeing Bhagavat coming from afar off, he prepared to one side a seat, a bath for his feet, and a footstool, and then he went forward to meet him, carrying his robe and his alms-bowl.

When Bhagavat's feet had been washed, he asked the Ayuchmat Rahula if there remained any water in the vase. The Bhadanta answered him that there was. "Well, Rahula, thou foolish man, who hast shunned the rules of virtue (who hast lied), thou art like that (dirty water left in the basin), I declare! He who knowingly tells lies, who is immodest, without shame, and who repents him not, is cast out of the priesthood, as is thrown away this (dirty water)."

This story is particularly interesting from the fact that it gives us a second version of the sermon to Rahula on lying, which sermon is mentioned in the Babra inscription of Asoka, where he says: "Thus, my lords, I honour in the first place these religious works—'Summary of Discipline,' 'The State of the Just,' 'The Terrors of the

[1] See Beal's Chinese Pilgrims, p. 82.

Future,' 'The Song of the Wise,' 'The Sutra on Conduct Befitting the Wise,' 'The Questions of Upatissa,' 'The Admonition to Rahula concerning Falsehood, uttered by the Blessed Buddha.'"[1] The Chuh-yau King agrees, I believe, with the Tibetan text and Comment.

Verse 11, ch. xi. p. 47.

"*Though one's hair may be grey,*" &c.

Bhagavat was residing in the Veratya (Virâta?)[2] country, near the Virâtanda (?). A Brahman of Virâta, a hundred years old and very decrepit, went noisily up to Bhagavat, and seizing him by the hem of his cloak, said to him: "Bho, Gautama,[3] when you see very aged persons why do you not show them respect? why are you not reverential? why do you not rise from your mat and offer it to them?" &c. "Because among gods and men I have not found a real Brâhmana." "But those, Gautama, are immaterial (*ro-med*) beings, among such as I, who are not immaterial, who do you consider a (real) Brâhmana?" "He who has cast away all the allurements of form and desire, who has no worldly goods, who has not to re-enter the womb, who is free from the skandhas of regeneration." "It is as if a Brahman had setting a lot of hen's eggs, and as soon as the chicks commenced to peck and to scratch at the shell he destroyed them." "But, Gautama, I am an old man—an elder!" "I, who have destroyed all the eggs in which ignorance showed itself—I am an elder for the whole world. Though one's hair may be grey," &c.

---

[1] See Rhys David's Buddhism, p. 224.

[2] Virâta was about thirty-six leagues west of Mathura. See Hiouen Thsang, iii. p. 336.

[3] *Kye Gautama*, equivalent to "Say, Gautama."

Verses 3 and 4, ch. xvi. p. 70.

"*By application and diligence,*" &c.

In Kosala a great number of Brahmans and householders were seated together in the playhouse (*Uad-mossai khang-pa-na*), as it was their custom to do now and then, to converse together. "Who are the beings," some one asked, "who will pass beyond birth and death?" A severe ascetic answered: "They who remain seated (for a long time) in one place (*stegs*)." Another said: "They who make sacrifices and burnt-offerings." Then Bhagavat said: "What think you, Brahmans and citizens (grihapati), if a dense forest or thick jungle had caught on fire and had (afterwards) been soaked by rain (and put out), would it grow again?" "Certainly, Venerable one." "And why so?" "Because the roots have not been destroyed." "Well, so it is with those who practise severe asceticism, or who remain seated (motionless), (passions will spring up afresh), because they have not completely destroyed attachment." And then he spoke these two verses.

Verses 3 and 4, ch. xviii. p. 78.

"*Fear is born of the forest (of ignorance),*" &c.

In Râjagriha there lived two Brahmans, Nala and (his wife) Upanala. After a while Upanala brought forth a very fine-looking child. A very wise soothsayer, who saw the child a short time after (its birth), was displeased with the signs (he saw on it), in consequence of which he made sacrifices, &c., to call Brahmâ. "What do you want?" (Brahmâ asked). "I want a long life for my son" (the father said). "I am not able to ensure that," he answered, "but the great Rischis know how;" and with that Brahmâ vanished. When they had heard this, they invoked with sacrifices the great Rischi Himavatapuschpa, an ascetic with great magical powers. So he also came, and having taken the child, he carried him off to his cell, where he became (in course of time) eminently learned and worthy of homage. Once Yâma, the lord of death, appeared among the holy students, and admonished them that in seven days they must die. "We have overcome your power," they answered. Yâma answered: "You have not the power of the Holy One. When one, having been with the Buddha Bhagavat, who is living in the land of Vâranari, has become one of the elect (Ariyas), then he can rely on himself." Then the five-hundred Rischis rose up in the air, after having produced (by magic?) two great kesara trees to protect them from the heat of the sun, they went to hear the dharma. When the young Rischis heard the first words of Bhagavat's sermon, they threw away one tree, and when they had heard the latter part, they threw away the other one; on hearing the middle part, they all threw themselves to the ground. The sermon was the verses given above.

Verse 19, ch. xx. p. 89.

"*He who is controlled,*" &c.

I have thought it advisable to reproduce the following anecdote, as it recurs with slight changes in the "Sûtra in 42 sections," section vii. Several other stories are given in the Commentary which resemble to a certain degree those of this sûtra, but none as closely as this. It must be borne in mind that the "Sutra in 42 sections" is also a compilation.[1] Both works most likely drew from the same source.

The son of a Brahman called Venggika (*sic*) came to where Bhagavat was, and spoke many angry words to

---

[1] See Léon Feer in the introduction to his translation of this work, and especially M. Beal, Four Lectures, p. 5.

him. He answered him, "Son of a Brahman, when the nakchatra that presided over your birth is near, do you pay your respects to your relatives?" "I pay them my respects, Gautama," he answered. "Son of a Brahman, if your relatives do not accept your homages, whose would they be?" "My own." "So likewise when any one speaks many sinful words to the Tathâgata, Arhat, the Perfectly Enlightened one, the Tathâgata accepts them not." "Çramana Gautama, I had heard from old Brahmans that if I went to the Tathâgata, the Perfectly Enlightened one, though I lavished the vilest abuse on him, he would not be angered, and here you are angry, Gautama!" Then Bhagavat spoke this verse.

Verse 1, ch. xxi. p. 90.

I translate the following lines to show how very nearly the Commentator follows the received Pâli version of the events that occurred shortly after Gautama had become a Buddha. "When he (Bhagavat) had obtained perfect enlightenment, Brahmâ, the lord of the universe, humbly begged of him to teach the dharma. Then the great Muni thought, "To whom shall I first teach the law?" Rudraka had died seven days before that moment; Arâṭa Kâlâma had also passed away. Then he thought, "I will teach the five." So Bhagavat started for Varâṇasi, and on his way, an Adjîvaka saw Bhagavat, and said to him, "Ayuchmat Gautama, your senses (appear) composed, your complexion is clear, your garments clean; who is your master (upâdhyaya)? Ayuchmat, to what sect do you belong? In what doctrine do you find pleasure?" Then he answered, "I am the Djina who has conquered Mâra (the evil one)!" "Then, Ayuchmat Gautama, you say that you are the Djina?" "The

o

Djinas are all like me," he answered. "Where are you going, Ayuchmat?" "I am going to Varânasi," &c.

It is a fact worthy of remark that throughout the Commentary, wherever the events related occurred shortly after the acquirement of Buddhaship, the Tibetan text is an exact translation of the Pâli text of the Mahâvagga. This, however, is easily explained from the fact that all the historical or legendary passages of the Commentary are derived from the Vinaya, the sûtras being only used to explain the precepts dogmatically, and the two versions of the Vinaya agree to a far greater extent, as far as they have been compared, than any other parts of the canons.

Verse 23, ch. xxix. p. 145.

"*Having killed father and mother,*" &c.

There lived in a certain mountainous district a very daring man, who having conceived the idea of becoming king, cruelly put to death his father, mother, the king, two pure Brahmans, and a great many inhabitants of the country, and then made himself king. Then he thought, "I will go to Bhagavat and question him; if he approves of my conduct, I will be very glad, and I will not destroy the vihara, and will do him many other good services." He did accordingly, when (Bhagavat) answered him (the words of the text), which when he had heard, he believed, and became a great householder (dânapati?).[1]

The sûtras teach that ignorance (avidyâ) is the root

---

[1] This first part is rather obscure, but I do not see that anything more can be made of the text. It evidently teaches that Bhagavat by the diplomatic way in which he answered a bloodthirsty tyrant, gained him over to his cause.

from which springs existence; that the sanskâra is caused by ignorance. Then again ignorance produces transmigration, as the "mother" produces the child; if it is possible to put an end to it (ignorance), it (transmigration) cannot exist.

"Father" means the component parts of the sanskâra, because actions (*las*) are born of the external world.

"King" means thought (vidjâna, fifth skandha); this word is used to imply that vidjâna is a cause (hetu) of the sanskâra. Râja, *i.e.*, "king," means also the region of passions, of form, and so forth.

"Two pure" means the component parts of form (rûpa), which term comprises the different forms of bodies.

"Kingdom" means the six senses (âyatanas), because they belong to the kingdom of vidjâna (thought).

"And its inhabitants" means feeling (sparcha) and perception (vedanâ), because they are the foremost and principal members of the six internal senses.

When one has put an end to these, the cause of existence and its consequences are at an end, done away with, and therefore "a man will be pure."

Now the Ariya Kâtyâyana explains the teaching of the sûtras as follows: The true cause of existence is desire (trichnâ); it is "the mother," for it is by reason of desire that beings are created; to conquer it is to get rid of an enemy.

The "father" is corruption (âsrava), existence, and deeds. The deeds which one has done, whether they be virtuous or corrupt, must be endured by the individual when they have matured; this is what the sûtras say.

The "king" means attachment (upâdâna) and the other perceptions of the mind, the six senses which are lord of the abode; this is what the âgamas (*lung*) say.

The "two pure" means essentially correct opinions

(darçâna), virtue (çîla), and diligence (vrata, or good behaviour).[1]

"Kingdom" means the region of sin (kleçâ).

"The inhabitants," what accompanies sin, and so forth.

He who has been able to gain the victory over all these enemies is "pure," for he has cast off all the objects of perception (*yul*). He is without impurity, for he is not in the same condition as those in this world. That is what he (Kâtyâyana) teaches.

Mr. Beal informs me that according to the Chinese Comment on this verse, "father and mother" means lust; "king and two important personages" implies arrogance and all its germs; "kingdom," the fetters of lust and arrogance.

---

[1] This agrees with the Chinese Commentary to a certain extent. It explains it by "the rules of the vinaya and heretical teaching."

VASUBANDHU'S GATHASAMGRAHA.[1]

PRAISE BE TO MANJUÇRI KUMARBHŪTA.

Thou chief of beings, in the region of the gods and on the earth there is no other great Çramana like unto thee! There is none in this world, neither is there any in the domain of Vaiçravana! Neither is there any in the highest regions of the abode of the gods, or in the regions below, or in the regions above. On the mountains and in the forests of the whole face of the world, where ere one goes, there is not thy like!

1.

They who go to the Buddha for a refuge, who day and night keep their minds continually reflecting on the Buddha, they have the profits of mankind.[2]

2.

They who go to the law for a refuge, who day and night keep their minds continually reflecting on the law, they have the profits of mankind.

3.

They who go to the church for a refuge, who day and

---

[1] According to the text of the Bstan-hgyur, the title of this work is "Çastrangātha Samartha." Immediately following, in the same volume, this work is reproduced with the Commentary, and here the title given to it is "Çastrangātha Samgraha."

[2] *De dag mi-yi rñed-pa yin*, literally "they of mankind are the profit" (diese sind ein gewinn der Menschheit--Schiefner). But according to the Commentary (fol. 250a) it implies that those men will find the four kinds of profits that men can obtain, viz., virtue, great joy, meditation (samādhi), and perfect purity. They are "the four perfections of mankind."

night keep their minds continually reflecting on the church, they have the profits of mankind.

4.

Doing what is virtuous, not doing what is sinful, he who follows the teaching of the wise men of old has never any fear of the lord of death: he goes to the other shore in the vessel of the doctrine.

5.

All the worlds are shaky, all the worlds are agitated, all the worlds are burning, all the worlds are full of smoke.

6.

Where there is no shaking, no agitation; where there is no association with humanity, where there is no trace of Mâra, there one's mind finds true delight.

7.

They who have shown the Victorious one (Djina), the guide, even the most minute mark of respect, will obtain, after having gone through the different heavens, the abode where there is no death (nirvâṇa or amatampadam).

8.

They who in this world dwell in forests, who are dispassionate, and who live a life of holiness, who take but a single meal a day, how will they be purified?

9.

By having no fondness for the past, by finding no delight in the future, by having found the present in this world, reflective through wisdom and discriminative, they put an end (to sinfulness), and in this way are they purified.

10.

Delighting in the law, rejoicing in the law, keeping his mind on the law, reflecting (or remembering) the law, a Bhixu will not fall away from the law.

APPENDIX.

11.

The wise man who in the life of the world has gained faith and wisdom has the greatest treasure, compared with which other treasures are contemptible.

12.

He who abides in the law, who is perfectly virtuous, who knows how to be modest, who speaks the truth, and who acts (accordingly) himself, in him mankind rejoice.

13.

By listening one learns the (different) parts of the law; by listening one turns away from sin; by listening one casts off what is not profitable; by listening one finds nirvâṇa.

14.

Do nothing sinful, observe most perfect virtue, thoroughly control your mind: this is the doctrine of the Buddha.

15.

One should do what is virtuous: if one does not what is virtuous, he has suffering; he who has done what is virtuous, in this world and in the other he will find joy.

16.

Speak the truth, refrain from anger, give to him who begs, though it be but a little: by observing these three precepts one will go (to dwell) among the gods.

17.

The reward of virtue is happiness: when one follows up his design to completion, he will speedily obtain blessed enlightenment (bodhi) and nirvâṇa.

18.

By charity one greatly increases one's merit; by perfect control one retains no enemies; by being virtuous one casts off sin; by putting an end to corruption (kleçâ) one leaves sorrow behind (nibbuta).

19.

He who, though wearing jewels, lives according to the law, who is controlled and who strictly lives a life of holiness (brahmacharya), who has cast off all the punishments of mankind, he is a Brâhmana, a Çramana, he is a Bhixu.[1]

20.

Faith, modesty, virtue, and charity, these virtues (dharma) holy men do praise: by this road one goes to the region of the gods, they say; this leads to the world of the gods.

21.

They (the bodies) are thrown away and scattered in every direction, like those pigeon-coloured bones; what pleasure, then, is there in looking at them?

22.

Alas! created things are impermanent; being born, they are subject to destruction; what has been born will be destroyed; happy they who are at rest.

23.

The end of all that has been gathered together is to be destroyed; the end of what has been raised up is to fall; the end of meeting is separation; the end of life is death.

24.

May the world be happy; may the years be prosperous, the harvests be plentiful, and may the law reign supreme; and may maladies and all other visitations be at an end!

Vasubhandhu's Çâstrangâthâsangraha is finished.

---

[1] Comp. Ud. ch. xxxiii. v. 1.

INDEX.

The Fa-kheu-pi-u is the text translated by Mr. Beal in his "Texts from the Buddhist Canon, commonly known as Dhammapada," Trübner's Oriental Series, 1878. The numbers of the Sutta Nipâta refer to the translation of M. Fausböll in the "Sacred Books of the East," vol. x.

Dhammapada.	Udânavarga.	Fa-kheu-pi-u.	Sutta Nipâta.
Chap.	Chap.	Page.	Verse.
I. 1	XXXI. 23	63	...
— 2	— 24	64, 169	...
— 3	XIV. 9	...	...
— 4	— 10	...	...
— 5	— 11	...	...
— 7	XXIX. 15	...	...
— 8	— 16	...	...
— 9	— 7	...	...
— 10	— 8	...	...
— 11	— 3	64	...
— 12	— 4	...	...
— 13	XXXI. 12	64	...
— 14	— 14	—	...
— 15	XXVIII. 33	...	...
— 16	— 35	67	...
— 17	— 37	—	...
— 18	— 39	—	...
— 19	IV. 22	—	...
— 20	— 23	...	68
II. 21	IV. 1	...	...
— 22	— 2	...	...
— 23	— 3	...	...
— 25	— 5	...	...
— 28	— 4	...	...
— 31	— 28	...	...
— 32		...	...
III. 33	XXXI. 8	...	...
— 34	— 2	...	...
— 35¹	— 1	...	...
— 40	— 35	73	...
— 41	I. 36	—	...
42	XXXI. 10	—	...
— 43	— 11	—	...

Dhammapada.	Udânavarga.	Fa-kheu-pi-u.	Sutta Nipâta.
Chap.	Chap.	Page.	Verse.
IV. 44	XVIII. 1	75	...
— 45	— 2	—	...
— 46	— 18	—	...
— 47	— 13	...	...
— 48	— 14	...	...
— 49	— 7	...	...
— 50	— 8	...	...
— 51	— 6	...	...
— 53	— 11	76	...
— 54	VI. 16	—	...
— 55	— 17	—	...
— 56	— 18	—	...
— 57	— 19	—	...
— 58	XVIII. 9	—	...
— 59	— 10	—	...
V. 60	I. 19	...	...
— 61	XIV. 15	...	46
— 62	I. 17	77	...
— 63	XXV. 22	—	...
— 64	— 13	78	...
— 65	— 14	—	...
— 66	IX. 12	—	...
— 67	— 13	—	...
— 68	— 14	—	...
— 69	XXVIII. 18	—	...
— 70	XXIV. 19	...	...
— 71	IX. 16	...	...
— 72	XIII. 2	173	...
— 73	— 3	...	...
— 74	— 4	...	...
— 75	— 5	78	...
VI. 78	XXV. 3	...	...
— 80	XVII. 11	...	...
— 81	XXIX. 52	...	...
— 82	XVII. 9	79	...
— 85	XXIX. 36	—	...
— 86	— 37	...	...
— 89	XXXI. 39	...	...
VII. 91	XVII. 1	...	...
— 92	XXIX. 24	...	...
— 93	— 25	...	...
— 98	— 18	82	...
— 99	— 17	—	...
VIII. 100	XXIV. 1	...	...
— 102	— 2	86	...
— 103	XXIII. 3	—	...
— 104	— 4	...	...
— 105	— 5	...	...
— 107	XXIV. 17	87	...
— 108	— 34	89	...
— 110	— 3	...	...
— 111	— 5	...	...
— 112	— 4	...	...
— 113	— 6	...	...
— 114	— 9	...	...
— 115	— 10	...	...

INDEX.

Dhammapada.	Udânavarga.	Fa-kheu-pi-u.	Sutta Nipâta.
Chap.	Chap.	Page.	Verse.
IX. 116	XXVIII. 23	...	...
— 117	— 21	...	...
— 118	— 22	...	...
— 119	— 19	...	...
— 120	— 20	...	...
— 121	XVII. 5	...	...
— 122	— 6	...	...
— 123	XXVIII. 14	154	...
— 124	— 15	...	...
— 125	— 9	...	662
— 126	I. 24	...	...
— 127	IX. 5	93	...
— 128	I. 26	...	...
X. 130	V. 20	...	...
— 131	XXX. 3	...	...
— 132	— 4	...	...
— 133	XXVI. 3	...	...
— 134	— 5	...	...
— 135	I. 17	...	...
— 136	IX. 11	...	...
— 137	XXVIII. 26	95	...
— 138	— 27	96	...
— 139	— 28	...	...
— 140	— 29	—	...
— 141	XXXIII. 2	97	248
— 142	— 1	—	34
— 143	XIX. 3	...	...
— 144	— 1	...	...
XI. 146	I. 4	99	...
— 148	— 35	—	...
— 149	— 5	—	...
— 150	XVI. 22	—	...
— 151	I. 29	...	..
— 153	XXXI. 6	...	...
— 154	— 7	...	.
— 155	XVII. 3	101	...
— 156	— 4	...	...
— 157	V. 16	...	...
XII. 158	XXIII. 6	104	...
— 159	— 8	—	..
— 160	— 20	—	...
— 161	XXVIII. 12	105	...
— 162	XI. 10	...	...
— 163	XXVIII. 16	...	...
— 164	VIII. 7	...	...
— 165	XXVIII. 11	106	...
— 166	XXIII. 9	...	...
— 169	XXX. 5	...	...
— 170	XXVII. 14	...	1118
— 171	— 16	...	...
— 172	XVI. 5	...	...
— 173	— 9	...	...
— 174	XXVII. 4	...	...
— 175	XVII. 2	...	...
— 176	IX. 1	...	...

UDANAVARGA.

Dhammapada.	Udânavarga.	Fa-kheu-pi-u.	Sutta Nipâta.
Chap.	Chap.	Page.	Verse.
XII. 177	X. 2	...	...
XIV. 179	XXIX. 54	...	...
— 180	— 56	...	...
— 183	XXVIII. 1	...	...
— 184	XXVI. 2	...	...
— 185	XXXI. 54	...	337
— 186	II. 17	160 (?)	...
— 187	— 18	160 (?)	...
— 188	XXVII. 28	112	...
— 189	— 29	—	...
— 190	— 30	—	...
— 191	— 31	—	...
— 192	— 32	—	...
— 193	XXX. 29	...	...
— 194	— 24	112	...
XV. 197	— 48	115	...
— 198	— 45	...	...
— 199	— 44	...	...
— 200	— 50	...	...
— 201	— 1	...	...
— 203	XXVI. 7	...	...
— 204	— 6	...	...
— 206	XXX. 27	...	...
— 207	XXV. 24	...	...
— 208	— 25	...	...
XVI. 210	V. 5	...	...
— 211	— 7	...	...
— 212	— 1	119	...
— 214	II. 3	—	...
— 215	— 2	—	...
— 217	V. 25	—	...
— 219	— 21	—	...
— 220	— 22	—	...
XVII. 221	XX. 1	—	...
— 222	— 21	—	...
— 223	— 18	—	...
— 224	— 15	—	...
— 225	— 19	—	...
— 227	XXIX. 48	122	...
— 228	— 49	—	...
— 229 ⎱	— 51	—	...
— 230 ⎰			
XVIII. 238	XVI. 3	...	...
— 239	II. 10	...	962
— 240	IX. 19	...	...
— 244	XXVII. 2	...	...
— 245	— 3	...	...
— 249	X. 12	...	...
— 250	— 13	...	...
— 251	XXIX. 40	...	...
— 252	XXVII. 1	...	...
XIX. 260	XI. 11	127	...
— 261	— 12	—	...
— 262	— 10	—	...
— 264	— 13	128	...
— 265	— 14	—	...

INDEX.

Dhammapada.	Udânavarga.	Fa-kheu-pi-u.	Sutta Nipâta.
Chap.	Chap.	Page.	Verse.
XIX. 266	XXXII. 18	...	...
XX. 273	XII. 4	...	...
— 274	— 11	...	...
— 276	— 9	...	...
— 277	— 5	...	...
— 278	— 6	...	...
— 279	— 7	...	...
— 280	XXXI. 32	...	...
— 283	XVIII. 3	...	...
— 284	— 4	...	...
— 285	— 5	...	...
— 286	I. 38	...	...
— 288	— 39	132	...
— 289	— 40	...	...
XXI. 290	XXX. 32	...	...
— 291	— 2	...	...
— 294	XXXIII. 70	...	...
— 295	— 71	...	...
— 296	XV. 12	...	...
— 297	— 13	...	...
— 298	— 14	...	...
— 299	— 18	...	...
— 300	— 21	...	...
— 301	— 22	...	...
— 304	XXIX. 19	...	...
XXII. 306	VIII. 1	...	661
— 308	IX. 2	...	...
— 309	IV. 13	...	...
— 310	— 14	...	...
— 311	XI. 4	...	...
— 312	— 3	...	...
— 313	— 2	...	...
— 315	V. 17	141 (?)	...
— 316 } — 317	XVI. 4	...	...
XXIII. 320	XXIX. 21	144	...
— 321	XIX. 6	—	...
— 322	— 7	—	...
— 323	— 8	—	...
— 325	XXIX. 13	132	...
— 326	XXXI. 5	—	...
— 327	IV. 26	—	...
— 328	XIV. 13	...	44
— 329	— 14	...	45
— 330	— 16	...	...
— 332	XXX. 23	...	...
— 333	— 22	...	...
XXIV. 334	III. 5	148	...
— 335	— 10	...	...
— 336	— 11	...	...
— 337	— 12	150	...
— 338	— 18	148	...
— 339	XXXI. 29	—	...
— 340	III. 17	...	...
— 341	— 14	...	...

Dhammapada.	Udânavarga.	Fa-kheu-pi-u.	Sutta Nipáta.
Chap.	Chap.	Page.	Verse.
XXIV. 342	III. 6	...	...
— 344	XXVII. 26	148	...
— 345	II. 5	—	37
— 346	— 6	—	...
— 347	I. 13	152	...
— 348	XXIX. 59	—	...
— 354	XXVI. 33	...	...
— 356	XVI. 15	...	...
— 357	— 16	...	...
— 358	— 17	...	...
— 359	— 19	...	...
XXV. 362	XXXII. 8	...	...
— 364	— 9	...	326
— 365	— 1	...	...
— 366	— 2	...	...
— 367	— 33	...	861
— 369	XXVI. 12	...	...
— 371	XXXI. 31	...	...
— 372	XXXII. 28	...	...
— 373	— 10	...	...
— 374	— 11	...	...
— 375	— 7	...	337
— 377	XVIII. 12	...	...
— 378	XXXII. 31	...	...
— 380	XIX. 16	...	...
— 382	XVI. 7	...	...
XXVI. 383	XI. 1	163	...
— 385	XXXIII. 26	—	...
— 387	{— 82 / — 83}	...	...
— 389	— 72	...	...
— 391	— 18	...	...
— 392	— 75	...	...
— 393	— 9	...	...
— 394	— 8	164	...
— 395	— 62 (?)	—	...
— 396	— 17	—	620
— 399	— 20	...	623
— 400	— 21	...	624
— 401	— 34	...	625
— 403	— 42	164	627
— 404	— 22	...	628
— 407	— 47	...	631
— 409	— 28	...	633
— 410	— 49	...	634
— 413	— 37	...	637
— 415	— 44	...	640
— 417	— 52	...	641
— 419	— 57	...	643
— 420	— 53	...	644
— 422	— 59	...	646
— 423	— 55	...	647

The following verses of the Udânavarga are taken from the Sutta Nipâta, and are not to be found in the Dhammapada. The numbers in brackets refer to the numbers similarly placed in M. Fausböll's translation:—

Sutta Nipâta.		Udânavarga.	Sutta Nipâta.		Udânavarga.
Uragasutta[1] 5	(5)	XVIII. 21	Kokâliyasutta 8	(659)	VIII. 4
— 2	(2)	XVII. 22	— 4	(660)	— 5
— 9	(9)	XXXII. 56	Subhâsitasutta 1	(449)	— 11
— 11	(11)	— 57	— 2	(450)	— 12
— 12	(12)	— 58	— 3	(451)	— 13
— 13	(13)	— 59	— 4	(452)	— 14
— 16	(16)	— 70	— 5	(453)	— 15
— 14	(14)	— 73	Sallasutta...... 3	(576)	I. 9
Kokâliyasutta 1	(657)	VIII. 2	— 4	(577)	— 10
— 2	(658)	— 3	— 1	(574)	— 13

[1] In Mr. Beal's translation of the Chinese Dhammapada (Fa-kheu-pi-u) we find, p. 164, a passage taken from the Uragasutta, though rather disfigured.

INDEX

TO THE

UDANAVARGA VIVARANA OF PRADJNAVARMAN.

N.B.—The numbers of the folios are those of the copy of the Bstan-hgyur in the India Office Library at London. The St. Petersburg copy is, I think, similar to this one. Vol. 71 contains 264 folios, and vol. 72 has 244 devoted to this work.

Chap.	Vol.	Fol.	Chap.	Vol.	Fol.
I.	Vol. 71 (du).	54a[1]	XVIII.	72	13a
II.	—	102b	XIX.	—	24a
III.	—	121b	XX.	—	30a
IV.	—	139a	XXI.	—	40a
V.	—	164a	XXII.	—	50a
VI.	—	178a	XXIII.	—	58a
VII.	—	188a	XXIV.	—	64b
VIII.	—	190b	XXV.	—	69b
IX.	—	198b	XXVI.	—	79a
X.	—	206a	XXVII.	—	100a
XI.	—	213b	XXVIII.	—	115a
XII.	—	221b	XXIX.	—	130b
XIII.	—	232b	XXX.	—	150b
XIV.	—	240a	XXXI.	—	175a
XV.	—	247b	XXXII.	—	193b
XVI.	—	256b	XXXIII.	—	214a
XVII.	Vol. 72 (uu).	6a			

[1] The first 53 folios of vol. 71 are devoted to the text of the Udânavarga.

www.ingramcontent.com/pod-product-compliance
Lightning Source LLC
Chambersburg PA
CBHW021402230426
43666CB00006B/609